THE
ENGAGEMENT
EQUATION

LEADERSHIP STRATEGIES
FOR AN
INSPIRED WORKFORCE

CHRISTOPHER RICE
FRASER MARLOW AND MARY ANN MASARECH

WILEY

John Wiley & Sons, Inc.

Contents

Preface: Standing on the Shoulders of Giants—The Legacy of Buck Blessing and Tod White

We often hear people describing employee engagement as a new field in corporate leadership. We beg to differ. Employee engagement—like innovation or effective management—has always been around. But it is an idea that leaders are turning to with more pressing attention as they explore all options for developing a competitive advantage. Increasing engagement is one of the few ways to boost productivity without additional headcount or new technology. While competitors can access capital, resources, and markets in the same way that you can, organizational culture and the engagement of a workforce are things that cannot be acquired or outsourced.

Two men who understood this were Buck Blessing and Tod White. In 1973 they founded their fledgling partnership above a barber shop in Princeton, New Jersey. Together, they devised a model of employee engagement and spent the next five years perfecting it by training thousands of professionals. To date, millions of people worldwide have benefited from programs that use this approach.

Sociology, psychology, and neuroscience are among the many disciplines that have taken a stab at the topic of employee engagement, and all have contributed to the body of research.

We have found that many of these suggested approaches are great in theory but fall apart when faced with the realities of implementing them in the workplace.

Our approach remains firmly as practitioners: we help organizations move the needle on employee engagement every day. The pragmatic lessons we have learned from advising senior teams and working hands-on in developing professionals around the world are distilled into this book.

Today BlessingWhite is a thriving consultancy and organizational development firm focused exclusively on employee engagement and leadership development. Companies such as General Electric, Toyota, Rolls-Royce, Unilever, Deutsche Bank, and Johnson & Johnson have turned to BlessingWhite to help craft their culture, develop their leaders, and engage their teams. In this book, we share the best practices and insights from these companies and many other organizations from around the world.

This journey began with Buck and Tod. We thank them for the initial spark and for starting us down the road. We dedicate this book to them.

Acknowledgments

This book was the work of many BlessingWhite colleagues around the world, past and present.

We want to specially acknowledge the contributions of David Koeppel, whose articles for the *New York Times* impressed us and made us realize we needed his guidance.

We are indebted to several of our partners in Asia Pacific—Ken Simper, Reg Polson, Rebecca Jones, Roy Gao, Ashish Arora, and Paul Mitchell—who arranged interviews with executives at companies in China, India, and Australia.

Our partners at Abu Dhabi University provided insight and arranged for us to talk to executives in the Middle East. We want to express our appreciation to Ahmad Badr, Gene Crozier, and Rabei Wazzeh.

We thank Paul Turner, Professor of Management Practice at Birmingham City University and longtime thought partner, for providing insightful guidance that kept us on track.

BlessingWhite employees in the United States and Europe contributed insight, challenged us, found interesting people for us to interview, did research and analysis, and made the book far better. Our thanks to Amanda Veinott, Matt Varava, Joan Dasher, Scott Mason, Chris Brunone, Eileen Garger, Charmian Hall,

Tom Barry, Bill Lingrel, Mike Shoenfelt, and Sue Kang, who got thrown in the deep end.

And finally, we wish to thank our editor at John Wiley & Sons, Adrianna Johnson, who guided us through the process.

—Christopher Rice,
Fraser Marlow, and
Mary Ann Masarech

Introduction

"We Accept the Premise"

There is an organization in your industry that enjoys the benefits of high employee engagement. You can read it in its performance metrics and feel it when you walk the corridors. You see it in the loyalty displayed by its customers, in its ongoing innovation, and in the piles of applications received for each job opening. This organization has achieved high levels of employee commitment and is buzzing with activity and a sense of purpose.

Is this your organization?

Maybe you are a leader in an organization suffering from chronic disengagement and are observing your more engaged competitors with envy. "How can we replicate what they have? How come they seem to have 'it' and we don't?"

High levels of employee engagement drive high organizational performance. As a leader you get this.

As you peel back the layers and examine the functions of that more engaged enterprise, it is difficult initially to put your finger on what exactly is different. Similar staff, similar expertise, similar products, and a similar customer base. But either the soul is there . . . or it isn't. How do you emulate or replicate those intangibles? And how do you protect and nourish it once you have it?

And so the conversation starts: if we want to tackle engagement, we first need to measure it. This requires time and money, and as in any rational organization the question becomes, "What is the payback?"

There are many studies on the benefits of having an engaged workforce. They proclaim direct lines between increased engagement and key business metrics. Promised benefits include

- Higher productivity
- More discretionary effort
- Faster time-to-market
- More rapid innovation
- Higher customer satisfaction
- Lower turnover
- Reduced absenteeism
- Fewer accidents
- More resilience to change
- Which all add up to . . . higher profitability!

Such studies, while academically stimulating, are totally useless to you unless you happen to have been part of that specific piece of research. Your enterprise has its own goals and strategy, its own strengths and weaknesses, and its own dynamics.

Meanwhile, consulting firms muddy the waters with dubious calculations on lost productivity and subjective definitions that are hard to act upon. Armies of bloggers and talking heads tout all kinds of quick-fix solutions, from free yoga sessions to recognition awards to engaging your employees with annual birthday gifts.

Despite the confusion surrounding the topic, most leaders agree—as Pat Hasbrook, a senior VP at global financial information services company Experian, once told us—"We no longer worry about calculating ROI for this. We simply accept the premise that an engaged workforce is essential for the success of the company."[1]

Spinning Plates

Picture if you will each employee as a spinning plate. You can see your organization as a large space with 100, 1,000, or even 50,000 plates spinning. Left too long without attention, they run out of energy, start spinning out of control, and may come crashing to the floor. Personal development, coaching, performance management, addressing team dynamics, and reinforcing objectives are all forms of plate spinning. Masters of this circus manipulation art can barely keep 100 plates spinning at a time.[2] How many plates can any harried player-manager handle? Typically, less than a dozen.

Low engagement is like having less energy flowing into these plates. The result is that more attention is needed to keep everything spinning. Leaders in organizations with low engagement describe it as driving with the brakes on. Things could be so much easier and get done so much faster if it were not for the drag caused by disengagement.

Managing in a low engagement environment is exhausting—and so is spinning plates. How often and how much time do you spend sweeping up smashed crockery?

An Individualized Equation

Here's another hitch: as a leader you can't actually *make* employees engaged.

Engagement is fundamentally an *individualized equation*. What might make one employee engaged might turn off the person in the next cubicle. There are many variables that can impact any one person's engagement. *You can't just become a better plate spinner. You have to find ways to keep the plates spinning on their own.*

To truly be engaged, people need to be satisfied with their immediate work and their career opportunities. *Work* and *career* are two intangible catchall terms used to describe something much more profound to employees: work is a very large part of an employee's identity. It is an opportunity to satisfy values, to maximize unique talents, and to learn, develop, and fulfill personal goals.

But your business's purpose is not to make employees satisfied. They also need to be contributing. Luckily for many of us, these are closely equated. Employees become satisfied *because* they accomplish results and know their contribution is recognized and adding value.

As we shall see, this is how we define full engagement: maximum satisfaction and maximum contribution. If you look at engagement through this prism, it becomes a win-win relationship. The individual is getting what he or she wants from the job, and the organization is getting what it needs from its employees.

A Long Road Ahead

The process of creating a more engaged workforce is not easy. According to industry analyst firm Bersin & Associates, 71 percent of organizations in North America measure employee engagement, yet only 35 percent of HR practitioners believe that their engagement efforts led to positive business outcomes.[3]

You *can* weave engagement into the fabric of your organization, but it *will not* happen next quarter and *should not* happen solely to improve the results of your upcoming employee survey.

Increased engagement is the long-term trajectory you will want to put your organization on.

The road is uncertain, but the returns can be great. The aim of this book is to wrap our arms around a concept that can sometimes be amorphous and bring practical solutions to the workplace. Not all workplaces are populated with highly engaged employees, but every organization can build—and sustain—a culture of high engagement. We will not sugarcoat it for you: it is a long road and demands sustained commitment from the executive team. But once established it will be the strongest competitive advantage you have.

If this is a commitment you are willing to make, we can show you the way. We share a practical framework to define engagement and the language to discuss it in practical terms. We articulate the roles that everyone in a workforce needs to play. We highlight the most productive strategies. We explain the pitfalls and lessons learned from those mistakes. And we challenge you along the way to ask yourself, "How engaged am I?"

Specifically, we will address how to

- Use a common definition and pragmatic framework for talking about employee engagement (Chapters 1 and 2).
- Lose your fascination with benchmarks and global trends and pay attention to the individualized engagement equations that are happening (or not) in every corner of *your* workplace (Chapter 3).
- Turn employee engagement into a shared responsibility and daily priority so everyone in your organization plays a role in solving the equation (Chapter 4).
- Take control of your own engagement. Dead batteries cannot jump-start others. If you are not fully engaged, your chances of creating a more engaged workforce are slim (Chapter 5).

- Build a culture to fuel engagement, and then protect it fiercely (Chapter 6).

- Create a crystal-clear organizational direction and work tirelessly to align all employees to that vision. If that is done correctly, they can take initiative and carry on (keep spinning) without endless intervention (Chapter 7).

- Open communication channels between managers and employees to ensure the constant dialogue required for employees to accomplish meaningful work (however they define it) while simultaneously driving your strategies forward (Chapter 8).

- Define what a future in your organization looks like by redefining notions of *career*. Then equip all employees to manage successful journeys (Chapter 9).

- Develop a realistic approach to assessing return-on-investment for engagement initiatives (Chapter 10).

- Avoid the many pitfalls of engagement surveys; your survey scores are not the prize (Chapter 11).

- Map out your entire initiative. Get started with best practices—whatever your size or checkered history with engagement initiatives (Chapter 12).

1

What Is Engagement Anyway?

> When the engagement you want isn't there, you don't need a survey
> to tell you that. You can feel it when you walk into the room.
> —*Keith Rodwell, group executive, BOQ Finance*
> *(a 137-year-old Australian financial institution)*

Critical but Elusive

Most people have experienced periods of full engagement at work. Yet as we have interviewed hundreds of executives and worked on engagement initiatives around the world, the lack of a common definition is striking. Ask one executive how she defines employee engagement, and you will get a vague statement about discretionary effort and motivation. Another might say it's about being in the zone or being married to the company. It is one of those experiences that is more easily described by engaged employees than defined by observers.

Ask those observers what engagement is, and you will still get disparate definitions. A problem with solving the mystery of employee engagement is that it's both critical to business success and elusive in its definition. But if we're going to move forward to discuss *increasing* engagement, we need to set up a common framework. First, let's consider some of the most popular definitions that don't quite work for our purposes.

Engagement Is Not. . .

Satisfaction Alone

In the early days of employee surveys, the primary focus was on satisfaction. Organizations wanted to know what kept their employees happy. For many this pertained to preventing union mobilization. As the Western economies shifted from industrial to knowledge economies, the emphasis of organizational practices shifted away from satisfaction alone.

Yet many of the research firms stuck with that initial definition, rebranding early satisfaction surveys as *engagement* surveys. The result, sadly, is that today many people still equate engagement solely with job satisfaction. This early misnomer gave engagement a bad rap in boardrooms as a soft concept, far removed from any business drivers. Some believed it created a workforce of happy, entitled, and potentially unproductive employees. Why would any fiscally responsible businessperson want that?

Common measurements of satisfaction that are restricted to benefits, work environment, and compensation (essentially a customer satisfaction survey for HR policies) set organizations up for failure. They reflect a transactional employer-employee relationship that is only as good as your organization's last round of perks or bonuses and cannot be sustained through market dips and organizational change. Psychologist Frederick Herzberg called these benefits *hygiene factors* that help prevent *dis*satisfaction, but do not necessarily *build* satisfaction. For example, increased compensation may not *increase* satisfaction, but unfair or inadequate compensation will cause *dis*satisfaction.[1]

Clearly, satisfaction alone is *not* engagement. If measured correctly, satisfaction *is* a critical ingredient.

Motivation

Some researchers point to theories of *intrinsic motivation* and encourage organizations to simply hire engaged (read, highly motivated) employees. This focus recognizes that engagement is not something your organization can do to its workforce. Having intrinsic motivation is a step in the right direction, because everyone in your workforce shows up every day with individual motivators, values, interests, and goals.

Still, employee engagement reflects a *relationship* between employees and employers, and as a result, *people cannot be engaged outside of the context of their job.*[2]

Commitment

Another mistake is to confuse the terms *engagement* and *retention* (even though they are closely linked). Most studies suggest that engaged employees are more likely than their disengaged colleagues to stay with the organization. However, many disengaged employees actually plan to remain—and do so for all the wrong reasons!

Engaged employees stay because they like their work—which is what they give to your organization in their engagement equation. The disengaged stay because of what they can get, such as financial rewards, career opportunities, job security, or comfortable working conditions. Intent to stay at a company, therefore, is not necessarily an accurate indicator of engagement. And retention of the wrong employees is simply bad business.[3] Being disengaged by no means indicates a total lack of commitment, but a commitment to the wrong things.

Let's move on to the definition of engagement that we'll be using throughout this book.

$$EE = MS^i + MC^o$$

Full employee engagement represents an alignment of maximum satisfaction for the individual with maximum contribution for the organization.

To understand this definition *and help make it actionable for you as a leader trying to increase engagement levels*, we need to explore the relationship between employees and employers.

The Playing Field: The Job

Jobs represent the intersection of employees' personal pursuits and your organization's interests.

MC° = Maximum Contribution

As a leader, you are no doubt aware of your organization's strategy for achieving success. That definition of success should be shaped by your organization's

- Goals, which reflect its mission (sometimes called a purpose or reason for being) and long-term vision (e.g., increased market share or specific financial targets)
- Core values or principles, which guide the decisions and behaviors of your workforce in pursuit of the organization's goals

In order for your organization's strategy to become reality, your employees must be willing and able to perform mission-critical tasks successfully. We call that *maximum contribution*. Jobs exist to drive your organization forward, to fulfill its mission, and to achieve its goals. In an ideal world, all employees deliver maximum contribution, but the reality is that on any given day, employees are, for multiple reasons, at different levels of job contribution.

News flash: what your organization needs for success is only half of the story and just half of the engagement equation.

MS^i = Maximum Satisfaction

Individual employees are on separate paths toward their own highly personal definitions of success. Sure, they need a paycheck. But they, too, have values, career aspirations, talents, development goal, and a need to fit their work into the broader context of their lives.

Unlike your organization's definition of success, there is no single definition of success shared by all employees. Individuals are all looking for work that works for them personally. We classify all those individualized interests under the label of *maximum satisfaction* at work.

Of course, employees, like your organization, don't always get exactly what they're looking for. They are achieving different levels of job satisfaction on any given day.

Engagement Happens at the Apex

Organizations are seeking maximum contribution from each individual toward corporate imperatives and metrics of success. Individual employees need to find purpose and satisfaction in their immediate work and have long-term visibility on a future with the organization.

The two are far from mutually exclusive and, in fact, feed off each other. The challenge for you is making sure that the mutually beneficial relationship is not left to chance, but managed skillfully to create sustainable levels of high performance. This is your engagement strategy.

At the apex of this model—(A) in Figure 1.1—*fully engaged employees are getting and giving the maximum.* Engaged employees

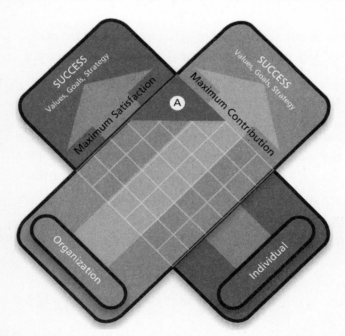

FIGURE 1.1 The Employee Equation. The top of the diamond is the apex. Full engagement occurs at the alignment of maximum job satisfaction and maximum job contribution (A).

are not just committed. Nor are they just passionate and proud. They have line-of-sight on their own future and a clear understanding of the organization's mission and goals. They are *enthused and in gear*, using their talents and discretionary effort to make a difference in the organization's quest for sustainable success.

We want to emphasize the word *sustainable*. Most organizations can generate bursts of contribution in the short term using approaches other than engagement, but these will be short-lived. Building a culture of engagement takes effort, but once established it will sustain high performance in your organization over time.

For an animated description of this engagement model, go to www.TheEngagementEquation.com/theX.

I Know It When I See It

Here are some of the ways leaders worldwide described this equation:

- "Employee engagement is about mutual effort: The company must work to engage the employees, but the employees must repay with contribution. We have a saying in China that you must dedicate yourself first before you expect dedication in return. That's a big part of our culture." —Ann Huang, senior HR manager, Red Star Macalline, China's largest furniture retailer, speaking about the win-win aspect of engagement

- "Having people stay with you is not a sign of engagement. There is always a risk of complacency in middle manager and senior manager roles. We see relatively

(Continued)

little turnover, and Indian companies can't face the idea of firing anybody after 10 years of service. In many ways it's a hangover of the caste system in the corporate world. What is needed at this level is a resetting of expectations, a recalibration." —Judhajit Das, chief human resources at ICICI Prudential, one of India's largest private insurance companies, describing the need for alignment and contribution, not just satisfied employees

- "People need to be compensated well but it is only one tool. At certain levels, as you progress in your career, compensation will not do it. Responsibility, new projects, and opportunities are more important." —David Norton, former company group chairman, global pharmaceutical giant Johnson & Johnson, on the importance of intangible motivators

Short-Term versus Long-Term Engagement

Engagement can fluctuate day to day based on the task at hand and events in the work environment. If it's a moving target, how can we refer to and act upon engagement? For the purpose of organizational engagement, we are talking about a mid- to long-term level of engagement: one that does not pertain to motivation around a specific task, but more in terms of an employee's relationship to his overall job. Each job will include enjoyable and productive tasks. It will also include less satisfying and less productive activities.

What we are interested in here is the balance for the longer term. Certainly when employees sit down to discuss career development or job satisfaction, they may have recent events top of mind. But with some encouragement, they will look back at the sum total of their contribution, their satisfaction, their working conditions, and their relationships. Employees will put up with specific less-captivating tasks if on balance their overall job is a fit for them.

Factors That Influence the Engagement Equation

There is a long list of variables that can influence any one person's ability to reach and sustain full engagement. Some can be controlled or influenced more easily than others because, as we described earlier, engagement is a complex, *individualized* equation. As a leader, you need to do your part, but always keep in mind that when we speak of an engaged workforce, it is really the sum of *each employee's* engagement.

If you want to learn more about why people are engaged—or not—you can spend days sifting through and comparing academic papers and the dozens of consulting firm studies.

You can also slice and dice your own organization's engagement data, conduct endless focus groups, and speculate in closed-door leadership sessions. You would only be contributing to today's engagement problem: too much analysis and too little focus on the practical tactics for *increasing* engagement.

In that spirit, we have chosen to highlight the most common factors that influence engagement as a foundation for taking action. The list is not meant to be exhaustive, but is in line with the common factors identified in most research in this area. According to one industry analysis, when it comes to engagement studies, "nearly all (89 percent) ask about career advancement, goal-setting and feedback, recognition and non-monetary rewards, and training and development in their surveys, suggesting that these aspects of work are the most common drivers of engagement."[4]

Given our definition of engagement as the alignment of maximum satisfaction for the individual and maximum contribution for the organization, we've grouped the factors into the two broad categories associated with those axes of the model—plus a third *other* category. This approach is useful but is by no means rigid. As you will see, some things drive both satisfaction and contribution. (Alignment with organizational strategy and mission, for example, supports satisfaction through a sense of belonging and meaning and contribution through clearly defined work priorities and expectations.)

Satisfaction

Compensation

You will quickly realize that we spend little time in this book discussing the role of compensation in engagement. There are a couple of reasons for this, but that is not to say compensation is not part of the picture. In a nutshell, compensation is an effective tool for *attracting* talent to the organization. It is also effective in helping *retain* people. Top talent will leave if, over time, their pay falls out of parity as their skills and experience develop.

When it comes to engagement, many studies have demonstrated that compensation alone (beyond a certain income level and as long as it is seen as fair) matters little. Nonfinancial engagement levers yield bigger long-term rewards at a much lower cost.

Career

Career development is often at the top of the list when employees are asked what will most improve their satisfaction. Yet items such as "I have career opportunities here" are often the lowest scoring of all in engagement surveys.[5] In response, many leaders think, "We have to create more jobs or provide clear-cut career paths," but it's not such a straightforward fix. When employees want support for their career, they may be looking for

- New challenges or experiences
- The acquisition of knowledge and skills
- Confidence that there is a future at your organization
- The next step in their long-term career aspirations (which may not be a promotion)
- Support in sorting through the many opportunities that they might actually have at your organization
- Someone to tap them on their shoulder and tell them what to do next

The last bullet highlights your challenge as a leader: everyone wants a career, but employees don't necessarily know what they—or their employer—mean by the term. And if employees are not clear on their personal definition of success, they will not be able to achieve it in your organization or any other. This is such a complex dilemma that Chapter 9 is devoted to it.

Job Fit

Job fit can be broken down into the work itself and the conditions under which the work is accomplished. Engaged employees like the work that they do because

- It satisfies their values and interests.
- It allows them to use their unique talents (and, therefore, they are successful).

- It is stimulating and provides opportunities to grow.
- It matters—to other parts of the organization, to customers, or to the larger community.

One way to describe this aspect of fit is *meaningful work*. Meaningful work is not an external definition of do-good jobs that save the world. It happens when employees find satisfaction and fulfillment in what they do every day. Do not overlook employees' relationship with their work because if someone hates what he does every day, no amount of inspirational leadership or recognition will make up for it for long.

A job's *conditions* determine how the work gets done. They reflect the organization's work environment and the particular requirements of a role, such as

- Control over how results are achieved
- Involvement in decision making
- Need for collaboration with colleagues
- Degree of formality (in dress code and office behavior)
- Hours of operations
- Manager involvement and style

Engaged employees have found roles or created situations that satisfy their personal values, work style, and current life outside of work. Their work *works* for them.

Of course, when we talk about *meaning, involvement, recognition, work/life balance*, and even *career*, keep in mind that these are intangible terms, like *beauty*. They are highly subjective and open to individual interpretation. For example,

- A project that would bore one person to tears might captivate another.

- A role that would meet one person's need for freedom, challenge, and growth might not fit someone else's need for a more structured, predictable work setting.

- A work environment that one person would find brutal might be exciting and stimulating to another.

So despite what you see depicted on television or in movies, there are very few truly bad jobs. The way employees feel about their jobs depends on their personal values, goals, and overall definitions of success at work. As your mother might have said when as a teenager you expressed disbelief at an unlikely couple walking down the street ("I don't know what she sees in him!"), "Every pot has a lid."

The implication for you as you build a more engaged workforce: the perfect match that fuels engagement requires the continuous efforts of employees, managers, your HR systems and practices—and it will change as organizational priorities shift and employee needs evolve. How many employees on your team are doing the exact same job they were doing three years ago?

Recognition and Rewards

If you have been in the workforce a while, you probably have a story of rewards or recognition gone bad—where an incentive program used as a short-term driver of behavior resulted in employees gaming the system or in the creation of unwanted side effects. Yet Derek Irvine, vice president of client strategy and consulting for strategic recognition firm Globoforce, explains, "Done right, recognition communicates the right behaviors, rewards and reinforces those behaviors, and gives a sense that the organization values employee contributions. Done right, recognition creates engagement."

Recognition helps employees feel valued and appreciated. Like career and job fit, it is highly personalized. Some people crave it. Others have a high tolerance for none—until they feel underappreciated. There also is a wide range of employee preferences for the kind of recognition demonstrated. For example, well-intentioned public praise for an employee who prefers to avoid the spotlight could be traumatic instead of a boost to satisfaction. As a result, recognition is most effective at the local level—planned by leaders who understand their employees.

Commitment to the Customer

Many employees spend years working in companies hearing about these mysterious customers whose expectations they aspire to exceed, but rarely, if ever, do they actually interact with one. All organizations are familiar with this disconnect, even those that have customer focus as part of their core values.

Yet exposure to external customers is a strong driver of engagement. It allows employees to see firsthand the value their own work creates, the purpose of the enterprise in action. Departments that are closer to the customer—such as sales, customer service, or consulting—tend to have higher levels of engagement than their peers, and when they do not, it is highly damaging to the business. The challenge for you: to find opportunities to expose back-office staff to end-users or customers to tap into this driver.

Contribution

Clarity of Priorities and Alignment with Overall Strategy

No new news here: employees need to understand what is expected of them so they can apply their talents and get the results your organization needs. When they have the added understanding of how their job fits into the organization's over-all strategy, they are better able to take initiative, make timely decisions, and be innovative. This connection to the bigger picture also helps fuel satisfaction through increased feelings of belonging and meaning.

The news flash, perhaps, is that most organizations fall short in aligning the daily priorities of employees with organizational strategy. Despite investments in scorecards and performance management processes and systems, employees end up working on the wrong things or find themselves out of the loop—and become less engaged. That means that if you think you have goal alignment and performance management covered, think again, and check out Chapter 7.

Resources and Tools

Engaged employees understand which of the 10 to-dos on their list take priority, *and* they have what they need to get their job done. Many believe that if they had even more resources, they would be able to increase their contribution.[6]

And whereas more resources will not necessarily increase satisfaction, insufficient resources will erode satisfaction, as this anonymous write-in comment from a survey illustrates: "We desperately need more resources. I enjoy my job 'in theory,' and I'm good at it. But I am BURNED OUT." In today's do-more-with-less work environment, it is even more important to be strategic with resource allocation.

Feedback and Development

This is another no-brainer driver of high performance. To achieve higher levels of contribution, employees need to

- Understand how they are doing in the tasks assigned
- Be conscious of the strengths they should leverage and the weaknesses that are liabilities (and therefore important enough to address)
- Find opportunities (through formal learning or assignments) to build the knowledge and skills that the organization needs now and in the future

But this is yet another basic human capital practice that needs improvement in many organizations. Well-intentioned managers know they should be coaching, but it is often at the bottom of their to-dos, or they are waiting for the right moment. And the once- or even twice-a-year performance management discussions are not enough to dictate the course corrections required for maximum contribution.

In addition, if you work in a high-tech firm or lead a group of engineers, scientists, highly technical professionals or creative ones, take note: expert employees exhibit a higher need for keeping current than the workforce at large, which places personal development high on the list of their drivers of satisfaction.[7]

Other

Immediate Manager

A lot has been written about people joining companies and leaving managers. Take a closer look, and you will find that employees flee *bad* managers. Despite popular viral videos of badly behaved managers, there is no epidemic. The majority of employees worldwide trust their immediate supervisors and have a decent working relationship with them.

Because of the way they are sandwiched between organizational imperatives and the people doing the work, managers are perfectly positioned to influence engagement by

- Helping employees clarify and then satisfy their personal drivers and aspirations at work
- Aligning the organization's goals with each employee's interests and talents
- Coaching and developing their teams
- Creating a team environment that supports maximum satisfaction and contribution

So all they need to do is find out where each individual on their team currently is, meet them there, and coach them to higher levels of engagement. This is easier said than done, so we will return to the critical role that managers need to play in the engagement equation throughout the book.

Senior Executives

Even though most employees can make it through a day, month, or even years without seeing senior leaders in person, top executives have a wide-reaching impact on engagement.

Executives set the overall tone of the work environment and the parameters under which the organization operates—not just in terms of processes, but most importantly in terms of organizational values. Their own behaviors are, of course, under a microscope, and a failure to walk the talk or hold themselves to the standards they set for the workforce at large will erode trust and deflate engagement levels. And ultimately, engagement drivers such as company reputation, brand integrity, and organizational culture, are shaped by executive decisions.

Organizational Change

As organizations respond to changing market conditions and customer needs, they reorganize, regroup, change direction, merge, or downsize. These changes, even if executed flawlessly, have an impact on employee satisfaction and contribution. For example,

- Reorganizations can alter reporting structures and manager-employee relationships.
- Shifts in strategy take time to communicate, which can cause confusion about the organization's directions and priorities.
- A merger may cast a shadow on career opportunities, require collaboration with new colleagues, or introduce new policies that alter job conditions and the work environment.
- New technology may redefine job requirements and the organization's definition of maximum contribution as well as employees' experience in getting the work done.

The World Outside

There are plenty of things happening outside the walls of your organization that are beyond your control, such as the global economy, broad industry trends, government regulations, local or national politics, and the behavior of competitors. These fall into that category of "Not being judged by what life throws at you, but by how you respond."

Although you can't change them, you need to acknowledge their existence and determine ways to minimize their impact. Whatever you do, do not fall into the trap of dismissing low engagement as a result of external forces. During the recession of 2008–2010 in North America and Europe, plenty of leaders rallied their workforce to higher levels of engagement and heroic performances despite the difficult economy.

Takeaways

- For engagement to be purposeful it needs to be defined in the context of a relationship between each employee and the organization. Only then can it be an integral part of your business strategy.

- We define *engagement* as maximum satisfaction and maximum contribution—the outcomes that both parties are respectively seeking out of this relationship we call the job.

- It is useful to understand the most common drivers of engagement as you consider how to create a more engaged workforce. Career development, job fit, recognition and rewards, customer commitment, clarity of priorities, alignment with the bigger picture, resource allocation, feedback and development, immediate managers, senior executives, organizational change, and forces outside your organization have an impact on how individuals feel about their work and how they contribute to your organization.

2

The Five Levels of Engagement

Alain Moffroid, vice president of customer development for Unilever, clearly recalls seeing his team members at their highest level of engagement: "I was tasked with introducing a new brand to Australia and New Zealand with a team that was made up of 30 young salespeople. This was a new product, so there weren't any sales yet. But they were passionate about winning. We were introducing Lipton Iced Tea for the first time and going head-to-head against Coke. The team had a very clear sense of purpose. The impact was enormous and the results were immediately visible," Moffroid says.

The team was facing a tough challenge, but its resilience was astonishing. Moffroid says that everyone on the team was valued and entrusted with the mission. They knew that the senior leadership had confidence in them.

Moffroid is unsure, however, if that kind of engagement and spirit can be replicated. While he would "love to re-create it," he says that engagement in smaller teams is easier. "Maybe it's that the clarity gets lost," he speculates.

The challenge that Moffroid faced is very common. Engagement is hardly static. Managers who have seen high engagement in their teams and enjoyed the tremendous results it engenders are frustrated when it slips between their fingers. *Fully engaged* is not a fixed state of being. Once it is realized, you can't check it off your to-do list and move on to another project.

If you're serious about engagement, it must stay on your leadership radar and be woven into your daily conversations. You need to stay aware of where your employees are—and not take high engagement for granted.

It Is Rarely All or Nothing

Depending on the study you reference, 50 to 70 percent of your workforce falls somewhere in between the extremes of full engagement and complete disengagement.[1] So it is useful to consider a broader framework.

Two Axes Are Better than One

It has been our observation that managers find a single-dimension measure of engagement less actionable. Often they are presented with team scores based on a scale of, say, 0 to 10, as popularized by Net Promoter Score. So they get a single metric along these lines:

By considering both contribution and satisfaction, the dynamics of engagement can move from a single dimension to dual dimension.

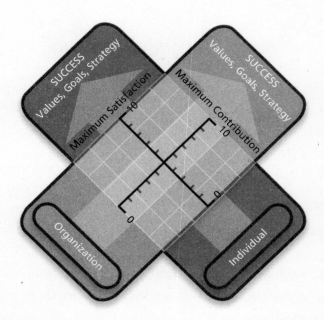

This allows us to look at a richer dynamic of engagement, based on a classic four-quadrant model (High-High, High-Low, Low-High, and Low-Low). Furthermore, we split the High-High quadrant in two, with the Engaged being defined as high on contribution *and* high on satisfaction.

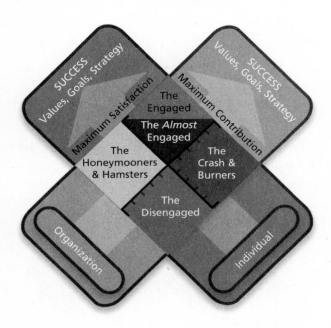

On any given day, your team and colleagues are scattered across the grid where individual and organizational interests intersect in five distinct segments. These segments are described by the two axes: contribution and satisfaction.

1. The Engaged: High contribution, high satisfaction
2. The Disengaged: Low contribution, low satisfaction
3. The Honeymooners & Hamsters: Low contribution, high satisfaction

4. The Crash & Burners: High contribution, low satisfaction
5. The Almost Engaged: Relatively high contribution *and* satisfaction

With this model in mind, managers are better equipped to meet team members where they are on the satisfaction and contribution scale, and to work with them one-on-one to help them progress toward full engagement.

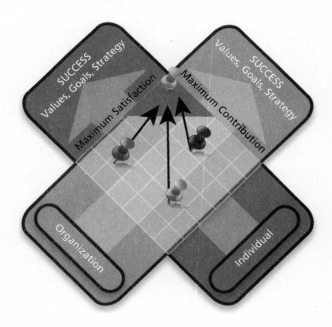

Let's take a look at what is likely to be going on in each of these five segments of the employee population.

The Engaged

Maximum satisfaction, maximum contribution.

Engaged employees are at the apex, where personal and organizational interests align. They are a subset of the top performers and contribute fully to the success of the organization. They also are getting what they need from work: satisfaction of their personal values and aspirations, emotional connections to the organization and to their colleagues, the right fit of employment with personal life, and the ability to use their talents to make a difference.

The Engaged are known for their discretionary effort and commitment. They are often the leaders (formally or not) in their workgroup. When recruiters call, the Engaged cordially cut the conversation short. Their work accomplishes both what's right for them and what's essential to drive your organization forward. They will also give you, as the leader, the benefit of the doubt more often than their colleagues: when something goes awry, they do not assume the worst.

Engagement from the Employee Perspective: More Great Days at Work

A quick reality check: all of our discussion of intangible engagement drivers, contribution, and satisfaction might produce yawns from your team. Ask them, however, about great days at work, and they perk up. Everyone has had a great day. Everyone wants more great days. And more often than not, an employee's great day delivers what the organization needs.

Tens of thousands of professionals worldwide have completed the Great Day at Work exercise that you will find in the Appendix. An employee will never say, "I had a great day at work last week when the network was down, so we couldn't deal with any customer requests. While it was down, I read a great novel at my desk."

The themes and best stories that emerge in interviews and group settings where this activity is conducted reflect elements of engagement that we've been discussing:

- *Challenging work:* Great days are often demanding days.
- *Community:* They often involve a team or other colleagues.
- *Talent utilization:* People are doing what they do best. They have to deploy and stretch their talents to achieve results.
- *Larger purpose and strategic alignment:* Something important gets accomplished that fits within the broader organizational objectives.
- *Results:* The organization and its constituents benefit.
- *Satisfaction of personal values:* Great days are often summed up with descriptors that reflect the things that individuals hold dear: achievement, recognition, integrity, personal development, or affiliation. The experience is individualized, even though there may be common elements across a group. One person's great day could be another person's nightmare.

Full Engagement Is Always at Risk

Full engagement cannot be taken for granted. Poorly communicated strategy shifts can create misalignment, rapid shuffling of priorities might zap energy, and a toxic co-worker can overshadow accomplishments. Major organizational changes (positive or negative) can impact engagement, especially if leaders do a poor job of communicating or putting changes in the right context. Life outside of work can evolve or take a dramatic turn.

All of these variables can result in a brand-new definition of personal or organizational success. Over time, a change in any one variable can cause your fully engaged employee to slip into a neighboring segment on the model or even plummet to the extreme: disengagement.

Moffroid of Unilever points to one such disruption: "Right now a big driver of disengagement is a wavering on strategy. It seems that alternating messages are being sent based on the last quarter's priorities such as top line growth versus profitability. Also the workload has been tremendous. Unilever has been asking a lot more of people in the last two years." If *maximum contribution* means driving sales one quarter and focusing on margins the next, how can an overstretched sales force connect to the goals?

The Disengaged

Minimum satisfaction, minimum contribution.

Let's be very clear: most disengaged employees didn't start out as bad apples, and they still may not be. Very few people actually show up at work with the intent to barely contribute while they miserably wait for their meaningless shift to end. However, research shows that the Disengaged are the most disconnected from organizational priorities. Their expectations of the job and of the organization are out of sync with their contribution. They know they are out of the loop, often feeling powerless, underutilized, and unappreciated. They are not getting what they want from work. They're not giving what your organization needs. It's a lose-lose equation.

The Disengaged are the most likely to say they plan to leave. If they did, the issue would resolve itself. The result would be positive attrition rather than the regrettable turnover you experience when a contributing employee departs. The problem is many of them don't leave. They stay for what they are getting in the employer-employee relationship (e.g., decent compensation, a likely bonus, the comfort of a job in an uncertain labor market, workplace perks, and job conditions that suit their lifestyle).[2] The more vocal Disengaged will collect a paycheck while indulging in contagious negativity. They have turned an emotional corner, and the longer they stay, the harder it is for them to move into a more positive place on the model.

The negativity of the Disengaged can lead to negativity in coworkers. Colleagues may listen to or overhear the complaints of a disengaged employee and start reevaluating their place at the company. An unhappy worker may seem like a singular problem, but the effects can ripple throughout a team. Mardi LePage, CEO of advertising agency URSA Clemenger, describes the symptom: "The Disengaged start to become a constant stream of criticism," she says. "As negativity creeps in, their colleagues are put on the spot. They now have to agree with the criticism or defend their colleagues and the agency."

For managers in particular, disengagement on a team presents a problem. Assuming managers are even aware of having disengaged employees on their teams, they are often at odds on how to deal with the issue. Employees confronted on their disengagement will often deny it. If the manager is not seen to take action on disengagement, she loses credibility in the eyes of other employees. In large organizations, managers dread the administrative hassle of firing somebody. A common cop-out is to trade the employee to other departments and pass the problem onto another manager. It is even easier to simply work with the more engaged team members, pick up the slack, and ignore the problem.

In teams where disengagement has become chronic, manager after manager can get chewed up and spit out. Often senior leaders fail to recognize the problem lies in the team and not the sequential managers they appoint.

Of course, in more extreme cases disengagement can lead to more than just low contribution. It can result in sabotage of the organization's effort—either purposeful or through the unintended consequences of the employee's behavior. The public displays of disengaged venting, amplified through social networking channels, have become the stuff of legend. In 2010, Steven Slater, a disengaged JetBlue flight attendant, made a dramatic exit from the airplane he was staffing (grabbing some beers and pulling the emergency chute) and became an overnight sensation on social media. But that sensation became a public relations nightmare for JetBlue. Likewise, the YouTube video of a couldn't-care-less FedEx driver throwing a brand-new computer monitor over a six-foot fence received hundreds of thousands of views.

The Disengaged may be the most removed from full engagement, but they are not lost causes. There are success stories of disengaged employees reinventing themselves as high contributors in new roles. But just a word of caution: these are the feel-good exceptions and will take the greatest effort to create. The Disengaged can be very vocal, becoming the squeaky wheel on your manager's cart. Investing tremendous effort to reconnect with a disengaged employee might be more effort than it is worth.

Invariably, the Disengaged are waiting for the last straw that inspires them to take action (and leave), the right opportunity to move into something new, or a well-meaning manager to rectify a bad situation. But they do need external assistance. If the Disengaged can't be realigned, re-inspired, and coached to higher levels of engagement, their exit benefits everyone, including themselves.

The Honeymooners & Hamsters

High satisfaction, low contribution.

Honeymooners are new to your organization or their role— and are happy to be there. They have yet to find their stride or clearly understand how they can best contribute to the organization's success. This status should constitute a natural, albeit temporary, holding area. But you can't assume that Honeymooners will figure everything out on their own. They need manager support and clarity of work priorities to join the ranks of the Engaged.

Rapid transition from Honeymooner to Engaged is critical in the first 90 days and is a function of (and sole purpose of) your onboarding process.

Hamsters are another more worrisome manifestation of high satisfaction, low contribution. If you've ever watched someone's pet hamster, you may have noticed it has two primary activities: running on an exercise wheel or snoozing in a cozy corner of its cage, half-hidden in the cedar shavings. There are parallel behaviors in your organization.

Some Hamsters are working hard but on nonessential tasks, contributing little to the success of your organization. They are, in effect, spinning their wheels. Eager Honeymooners without correct focus can turn into Hamsters.

It is possible for engaged employees to land in the zone of Hamsters because they choose to prioritize things that are no longer critical to the company mission. This can happen as workforces become leaner and organizations shift strategies to address rapid change or increased workloads. If your strategy changes and you don't communicate and realign, you are in effect creating an army of eager Hamsters: teams of people working on yesterday's priorities!

If left out of alignment for long, some hard-working Hamsters eventually figure out that their efforts have no impact, and they become demoralized, sliding into disengagement. Others may end up on the wrong end of the list when layoffs loom, surprised to learn that they were not indispensable. They were committed and talented, and represent a loss of huge potential to the organization.

Then there are the hardly working Hamsters. They are aware that they're not contributing much, but enjoy having a great job as opposed to doing great work. Some may have a few years left and can be considered retired in place. Some may have slipped through the cracks of a less-than-optimal performance management system as they do the work they like, instead of the work that matters. Others have been left alone by ineffective managers who are afraid that pruning dead wood might leave them with a reduced head count for an undetermined future. Some may be kept on staff, resting on the laurels of specific technical expertise they occasionally are called upon to provide.

And what is the future for these Hamsters? They're unlikely to slip into disengagement, but they are likely to have a negative impact on the engagement levels of their colleagues. Hard-working team members may need to step in to do or re-do the Hamsters' work. High performers who are rewarded with even more work might wonder with disgust why their colleagues down the hall are allowed to remain. Accepting visible low performance lowers the bar for the whole team. As with the Disengaged, dealing with Hamster behavior becomes a yardstick by which other team members will judge a manager.

The Crash & Burners

Low satisfaction, high contribution.

Crash & Burners are often your weary heroes. These employees are top producers who are not achieving their personal definition of success and satisfaction. They're giving but not getting in exchange.

In today's world of work, that someone may contribute strongly in the absence of personal satisfaction may seem farfetched. But as Dr. Gerald Ledford Jr., a consultant who specializes in human capital issues, points out, there is nothing to support the notion that job happiness equates with job productivity. It's quite possible to hate your job but, at least for a while, continue to be a high performer.

Crashing and burning, like the Honeymoon, can be temporary. It may be that there are insufficient resources, a consuming client project, or a departing colleague who leaves ghost work that needs to be picked up in the short term. During the 2008–2010 recession, heroics became the new normal in many Western organizations. A large portion of the workforce put aside their personal aspirations for the sake of the larger goal: the company's long-term survival. However, that scenario cannot be sustained.

Remember that individuals differ on the kind of change and workloads they can tolerate. A mountain of work does not mean instant crashing and burning. For some members of your workforce, it could represent a challenge that they live for—and full engagement can be sustained at least for a while.

"Workload only becomes an issue if the engagement level is not there," says Moffroid of Unilever. "People will work very hard if they are engaged, and it does not become an issue. People can thrive on 'positive stress.'"

Don't assume all Crash & Burners are overworked. Here are some other scenarios at that can lead to high contribution but low satisfaction:

- High performers with unmet career ambitions who become disillusioned when colleagues are promoted or obvious career opportunities are lacking
- Expert employees like engineers and IT professionals who are bored waiting for the next big challenge, dismayed when an exciting project gets tabled, disappointed that they have to work on critical but technically unchallenging work

(while less-experienced employees are put on bleeding edge projects), or frustrated when their thirst for development isn't satisfied

- Individuals with high recognition needs whose maximum contribution goes unnoticed and unappreciated (or worse, credited to others)
- Top contributors whose emotional commitment suffers when senior leaders misstep, or the organization struggles to deliver on its promises to customers, or sales objectives fall short because another division missed its target
- Employees who love their work and do it well, but need higher salaries or more flexible working conditions

One more observation to stress just how individualized the engagement equation can be: some employees who are Crash & Burners are their own worst enemies. They may be falling short of maximum job satisfaction because they have not clearly defined what personal success looks like for them. (Heed the adage, "If you don't know what you're looking for, you won't find it.") Some may be devoted to perfectionism or lack self-discipline in work habits, resulting in a job that takes up too big a portion of their lives. Others may be using work as an escape from an unenviable situation at home. These employees may never achieve maximum job satisfaction at your organization or any other. Their managers can't fix the situation. They can only provide candid, compassionate feedback and support as individuals own and resolve their personal challenges.

What ultimately happens to Crash & Burners? Some figure out (with or without their manager's help) how to get what they're looking for on the job and are able to move into the ranks of the Engaged or Almost Engaged. Others leave your organization in search of increased job satisfaction. As high contributors, they are sought after and highly employable. Many, unfortunately, quit and stay. They stop working hard and slip down the contribution scale to join the Disengaged. They may become vocal about poor leadership decisions or bad working conditions. Even when they're not criticizing or complaining, their colleagues often notice the change in their engagement level. These colleagues may (consciously or not) be brought down with these former stars.

The Almost Engaged

Relatively high satisfaction, relatively high contribution.

It's likely that on any given day, at least a quarter of your workforce is Almost Engaged.[3] These employees are among your high performers and are reasonably satisfied with their jobs. They may not have consistent great days at work, but they know what those days look like. And with a little help (greater clarity of focus, more resources, better understanding of their own needs, development opportunities, inspirational leadership, or meaningful recognition), they can move into full engagement.

The Almost Engaged, like the Engaged, are not plotting their departure. Unlike the Engaged, however, when recruiters call, they'll listen and are open to new opportunities. The Almost Engaged can be lured away because they're committed but not invested in a future with your organization. They're doing good but not great work, and they are highly employable. When a headhunter comes knocking, they will at least entertain the idea of a new opportunity.

The good news: the Almost Engaged have the shortest distance to travel to reach full engagement. The bad news: there is no buffer between them and the territories of Hamsters, Crash & Burners, and the Disengaged.

The Five Levels of Engagement in the Real World

Although it is useful to have a common language and understanding for how the five engagement levels play out in your workplace, this framework is merely a starting point. Engagement remains an individualized equation, reflecting each employee's personal interests, motivators, talents, and aspirations. These factors then mesh with his unique job situation, relationship with his immediate manager, and link to your organization's goals. Ten people can be at the same place on the model for 10 very different reasons.

As useful as these segmentation monikers might be to discuss levels of engagement, you should not label an individual a Hamster or a Crash & Burner. That just happens to be her current position on the job grid. But as we have already stressed, this level is subject to change—and it will vary over time depending on the job and changes in the variables. For example, the Engaged may drift into the Almost Engaged segment quite easily, and vice versa.

There is no one prescription to offer organizations for moving employees from one level to the next. However, there are strategies that you can implement to help ensure that the alignment of individual and organizational interests happens more frequently. The chapters that follow explore those approaches.

Takeaways

- Engagement is shaped by organizational and individual definitions of success. Full engagement will not occur if either definition is poorly clarified or communicated.

- Engagement is not static. Individuals move around the model depending on variables that are personal, managerial, organizational, and external. Full engagement, when it is achieved, can't be taken for granted.
- There is no prescription or magic pill. Two individuals may be experiencing low satisfaction and high contribution for different reasons. Your organization or your managers can't fix them with a broad-brush approach. Engagement strategies are based on meeting individuals where they currently are, helping them understand the variables that impact their own engagement, and then facilitating their transition to full engagement.
- By adopting a two-axis model that is based on contribution and satisfaction, managers can develop a more effective understanding of the dynamics of engagement by considering five different levels: Engaged, Almost Engaged, Crash & Burner, Honeymooners & Hamsters, and Disengaged.
- Everyone may benefit when your disengaged employees leave.

Global Insights and Macro Trends

In 2009, the world economy was caught in the death grip of a global economic crisis. Headlines proclaimed it the worst recession since the Great Depression. In the United States, unemployment reached 10 percent, and in some European countries, the jobless rate was closer to 20 percent.

Most companies were going into crisis management mode. They were trimming back on staff, canceling big investments, and nervously waiting for the next bit of bad news.

But in Skokie, Illinois, David Asplund, the CEO of Lime Energy,[1] was dealing with a different dynamic.

Asplund was in the middle of a turn-around, transforming this $16 million clean-energy company into a $95 million extremely profitable enterprise. Lime Energy was experiencing

104 percent annual revenue growth. In 2009, at a time when funding was scarce, the company raised fresh capital.

"In the beginning, we were really a start-up company, and it was difficult to attract the employees we wanted," Asplund explains. Specialized engineers are rare and in high demand. Lime Energy had to overcome early obstacles in finding the expertise they needed.

It was finally through geographic expansion and business acquisition that Lime Energy tripled its workforce (from 100 to 300 people) and found the talent it was looking for.

Unlike most CEOs at the time, Asplund was concerned about integrating recently acquired firms. Lime Energy was expanding when most companies were downsizing and losing staff.

While others were managing the downturn, Lime was focused on growth. Other executive teams looked to dispose of less productive business units, but Asplund was managing integration issues.

For Lime Energy, the "engagement zeitgeist" for the recession did not apply. Its leaders needed to manage their own specific business dynamic.

"Acquisitions are easy, but integration is the difficult part. There was always a tendency to have a 'them and us' attitude as opposed to being one, consolidated company," Asplund says. The different units, especially sales and operations, had to be pulled in toward one goal. While other firms were busy laying off entire departments, Lime Energy had several key people leave who felt they were not being represented.

■ ■ ■

There is a growing body of academic research around the factors that correlate with engagement, such as demography, geography, and industry. This research provides us with some useful broad categories to consider.

Engagement is *an individualized equation*. Applying demographic generalizations to any individual is a common pitfall, and employees do not conveniently adhere to stereotypes. We frequently interview employees who run counter to all general preconceptions. These can include disengaged senior executives, Gen Y employees who behave as if they were lining up for retirement, and young mothers who want nothing more than the opportunity to work longer hours. People will always surprise you, so you need to consider the individual, not the demographic.

The situation within your organization outweighs any and all external factors, including regional, generational, gender, or union membership. Whatever factor you choose to analyze, it will never be as useful to your understanding of engagement dynamics as having a firm handle on *your* culture, *your* objectives, *your* ability as an organization to communicate goals, and *your* ability to provide meaningful work and career visibility.

Just as David Asplund couldn't manage his business based on the headlines in the *Wall Street Journal*, you cannot weave engagement into your organization based on demographic generalizations. Broad trends can provide nothing more than a discussion framework to explore the dynamics of engagement.

With this caveat, let's look at some macro-trends of engagement and the factors behind them.

Starting at the Top

The higher up in the organization you go, the more likely you are to be engaged. In some regions, twice as many senior executives are engaged than individual contributors.

Most people find this to be obvious. But why is it obvious? Why should we assume that those people with broader job scopes, who hold positions of greater accountability, should be more engaged?

A number of factors may be at play here: greater authority and control over work, close proximity to organization direction and decisions, and the maturity to know (or to have figured out through trial and error) what's important to you and how to achieve it. Another possible factor at play is that individuals with the personal clarity and initiative required for engagement may be more likely to be consistently promoted.

That executives tend to be more engaged is an important factor in planning our initiatives for two essential reasons:

1. *Perceptions on engagement may be biased.*

Senior executives tend to either overestimate or underestimate the engagement of their team members because they project or contrast their own engagement levels to those of other employees.

We have seen engaged executives get frustrated by what they perceive as low levels of engagement in the organization. They ask, "Why can't they all be as excited as I am about the potential of our business?" But when we discuss the issues with the staff, we find that they are, in fact, highly engaged. They might not be *as engaged* as their boss, they might have some questions or reservations (which they feel uncomfortable expressing), but fundamentally they are *enthused and in gear*.

2. *The feedback executives receive is notoriously biased.*

Depending on the culture, they may either be told what they want to hear or bear the brunt of employee venting. Their perceptions of engagement are consequently biased. An executive typically has a good handle on her immediate team's engagement dynamics. But it takes conscious effort on behalf of any executive to get the real unbiased picture of what is going on in the rank and file.

Although senior executives as a group are more likely to be engaged than other employees, it is not unusual to find a third of senior leaders at a company are not engaged (and up to a half in poorly led companies)—still way more than you would want. And a disengaged senior manager has a far greater deflating effect on the organization than a disengaged front-line employee.

Addressing your own engagement as a senior leader is a topic we will discuss in Chapter 5.

Some Departments Fare Better than Others

Each organization will experience engagement pain points in different areas. But one notable trend is this: the closer a department or function is to customers or clients, the greater the likelihood that team members will be engaged. The same is true of departments that are at the core of the organization's strategy, such as the creative group in an advertising agency or the core programing team at a dot-com firm.

This stems from two dynamics:

The first is that those departments have the best odds for engagement. They are core to what the company does and their priorities are more explicit. They often see their work put on a pedestal and generally see a more direct relationship between their own personal output and the company's success. These groups are the first to be included in communications or consulted on a company's future direction.

The second is that low levels of engagement in those departments would prevent the organization from moving forward.

The organization invests in its best managers and focuses most of its attention on these groups. They are less likely to be a target for outsourcing and more likely to receive the resources they need to get the job done.

If this seems counterintuitive, just consider this simple hypothetical. If a VIP visits your company's head office or main production plant, what would you include on his official tour? It's unlikely that you will be showcasing the accounts receivable group. Unfortunately, the message this sends to that department is clear: you are not as critical to our success as your colleagues over in product design.

It has been a proven and productive strategy for companies to focus on core competence, a trend that has fueled the multibillion outsourcing industry, and this trend continues. The worldwide business process outsourcing (BPO) market is thought to have grown 6.3 percent in 2011 and could grow a further 5 percent in 2012.[2] As the BPO model gets refined, on both the supply and the demand side, many more non-core services are being outsourced. A natural result of this is to groom, reward, and promote more aggressively in those core departments. Functions seen as commodities are more likely to be asked "How can you do more with less?" and not "How can you contribute to the strategy?"

So, What Is the Risk?

Having lower levels of engagement in non-key departments may be acceptable. Energy and investments need to be channeled into parts of the organization that will yield the greatest return. It helps to be aware of this pattern and yet to realize that with the right managerial talent, a company can achieve high levels of engagement in non-core functions.

Companies That Choose to Outsource Entire Departments

There is an increasing trend in Western economies (some describe it as worrisome) of large organizations relying on contract labor for dealing with some of the less value-added tasks and more dangerous or low-paid work.

While none of these firms would openly admit to it, the strategy is closely connected to employee branding. Simply put, these companies develop two categories of workers:

1. Workers providing high value-added work. These are typically the full-time employees (sometimes contractors) who may receive full company benefits such as private healthcare benefits and pension plans.
2. Workers who perform low-pay, dangerous, and/or high-liability work. These are increasingly subcontracted functions.

There are several benefits to corporations:

- Using contract labor allows companies to rapidly ramp-up or wind-down activities around periods of peak activity (retail at Christmastime, agriculture in summer).
- They can more rapidly adopt new processes and technology, remodeling their workforce around these new methodologies.[3]
- They can keep a clean bill of employee-relations health, still win the best-places-to-work awards, and yet access large pools of workers who do not add to the benefits

(*Continued*)

overhead. These workers also do not require the same level of care and attention. It is easier to provide a pension plan for all your employees when half of your workforce is not actually on the payroll.

- They can bypass labor agreements or other dues of their social contract to reduce wages and benefit costs.

Many industries, encouraged by deregulation and lower unionization of the full-time workforce, have turned to this model:

- In an essay published in the *Week*, Mac McClelland describes the tough working conditions of warehouse workers, the pickers, who are hired by the tens of thousands in warehouses that are hundreds of thousands of square feet in size.[4]
- U.S. wireless carriers came under scrutiny for their use of subcontractors to eliminate the risks of managing wireless antenna crews.[5]
- Along the same lines, larger carriers in the U.S. airline industry have subcontracted to regional carriers to reduce the costs associated with tenured pilot contracts.[6,7]

The Generational Debate: Those Pesky Gen Yers

When Gen X broke onto the scene back in the era of punk rock, there was a lot of establishment concern that this unruly mob would never adapt to the world of work. The stereotypes that Gen Yers are labeled with today were also attributed to Gen X: disrespectful of seniority, lack of work ethic, little commitment to the organization, and certainly not good team players.

The new wrinkle is that Gen Yers do it all online, and this technological divide appears to increase the sense of alienation that Baby Boomers feel in dealing with their younger colleagues.

In our own research, we discovered that age does have a strong correlation with engagement: 23 percent of employees born between 1978 and 1994 are identified as fully engaged, and 21 percent are disengaged. Compare this to the Baby Boomers (born 1946 to 1964) in which we find 37 percent are engaged and 14 percent disengaged. Gen Y has lower levels of engagement when compared to the older generation.

But we have to ask,

- Are Gen Yers fundamentally different from previous generations, or are they just less experienced? Are their values truly different, or are they similar to those of people entering the workforce 30 years ago?
- Consequently, should organizations have fundamentally different approaches to engagement whether they are dealing with young workers or more tenured employees?

Take compensation. Do Gen Y employees expect unreasonably high starting salaries? According to Pew, in 2010,

> Less than a third (31 percent) of employed Gen Yers say they earn enough money to lead the kind of lives they desire. That judgment contrasts sharply with the majority of workers ages 46–64 who say they are satisfied with their current income (52 percent).[8]

But young people never think they have enough spending money. In a Pew Research Center survey conducted in 1997 during an economic boom, only three-in-ten adults ages 18 to 29 said they made enough to live the ideal life they wanted.

In the arc of most people's lives, income and earning power tend to be relatively low in those younger years and rise through middle age.

All workers in entry-level jobs, no matter when they entered the world of work, usually find their salaries are not enough to support their lifestyles. This is hardly a new phenomenon.

In her research for Bersin & Associates, Dr. Brenda Kowske notes,

> First and foremost, generational differences are small overall. There are a lot more similarities than differences, and where differences do exist, it is likely more due to life stage. . . . Any one Gen Yer might be substantially different than the research-driven description of the generation.[9]

Dr. Kowske adds that the generation an employee belongs to represents only 2 percent of the variability in engagement drivers. Consequently, if you do want to use demographics as a rule of thumb for your engagement initiative, generation is probably not the best starting place.

What does it mean if the drivers are similar, but the engagement levels are significantly different? The bottom line is that young employees who are new to the workforce are still trying to get acclimated. They are still learning how to make contributions, discover where their personal strengths lie, and determine what gives them satisfaction at work. Since they benefit from an overall work environment that permits mobility, they are taking the opportunity to try their hand at multiple positions to find out what works best for them. To them this typically means switching employers, but it doesn't have to be that way. Do not look down on candidates with diversified experience at several firms, but see this as an opportunity to help young talent forge a career within your enterprise by providing frequent new challenges and responsibilities.

The conclusions from our research and our work in organizations can be summarized as follows:

- Despite popular belief, the fundamental drivers of engagement and personal values of Gen Y employees are not significantly different from those of Baby Boomers or Gen Xers.

- Gen Yers grew up in a world of work that presents variables that previous generations are still getting used to. This includes the blend of personal life and work life, the adoption of technology at work and at home, and a less permanent social contract between employee and employer. They approach the world of work having fully accepted those changes. This is how the world works; in fact, to them, these are not really changes at all.

- Overall, Western societies are trending toward more geographic mobility, later (and fewer) marriages, and later (and less) childbirth. These trends mean that younger employees will commit to family later in life and therefore remain more mobile in terms of employment. For example, in the United States, "Millennials are more likely to be living with other family members (47 percent), such as their parents, than were the immediate two previous generations at the same age (Gen Xers, 43 percent; Boomers, 39 percent). They also are more likely than others had been at the same stage of life to be cohabiting with a partner or living with a roommate."[10]

- While Gen Yers may expect some differences in terms of modalities (such as communication channels, contemporary working conditions) or style, their engagement drivers do not differ. Just like their elders, they want clarity, purpose, and long-term personal development opportunities. The approach to driving engagement should not be fundamentally different between generations in the workforce.

Savvy employers see through the generational filter and acknowledge that all employees need the opportunity to articulate their own definition of success and gain clarity about organizational goals. They need to enter into a meaningful dialogue with their manager and to carve out a purposeful job that matches their strengths with the needs of the organization.

The Pew Research Center team agrees: drawing direct conclusions on generations is "too difficult because, try as we might, we know we can never completely disentangle the multiple reasons that generations differ. On many measures, the long-term trend data needed to make comparisons simply do not exist. Also, while generations may have personalities, they are not monolithic. There are as many differences within generations as there are among generations."[11]

Regional Factors

Regional factors are significant enough that we need to take them into account when addressing engagement, especially when it comes to global engagement initiatives.

In broad terms, we have consistently found Indian employees to have high levels of engagement (37 percent engaged in 2011), followed by North America (33 percent), then Europe (30 percent). China remains an outlier with only 17 percent of employees engaged.[12]

How should this—and other regional variations—inform your engagement initiatives?

First, regional factors do not supersede any factors specific to the individual or the organization. Organizations need to find solutions that work for them and address their needs, and allow for cultural and regional nuance to be taken into consideration.

This is especially true in the execution of any multi-region initiative.

Take the Landmark Group. Landmark is a $4.7 billion retail giant that operates out of Dubai. With 26 brands and 1,087 outlets worldwide, its footprint ranges from Egypt to China, with a concentration in the Persian Gulf region (United Arab Emirates and Saudi Arabia). Landmark operates over 100 stores in India alone.

While India and the United Arab Emirates have strong economic ties, their cultures are very different. Organizations in the Persian Gulf region have had less of a focus on employee engagement due to restrictive employment policies and a captive labor market. Landmark's operation in India could not afford to operate on the same basis. "As we evolved and the business started to grow rapidly in India, we had to capitalize on the processes we inherited from Dubai and also bring in innovative processes relevant to the Indian market," says B. Venkataramana, the Indian senior vice president and chief people officer of Landmark, who is based in Bangalore.

The Indian operation introduced onsite counselors, rewards and recognition programs, wellness programs, and other common good initiatives. It also worked on aligning employees and clarifying performance expectations, and transforming its career process from a formal, manager-led process to one where employees were encouraged to take the initiative.

The key takeaway from regional variations is this: if you see lower levels of engagement in any given geography, do not assume that what you did in a more engaged region will work everywhere else.

Understand what regional dynamics will impact your initiatives, and adapt on the ground to fit. Entrust local managers and regional leaders with adapting the process to local culture and work practices.

The Four-Year Itch

Employees tend to report high levels of satisfaction when they start a new role or join a new company. If a company is savvy at onboarding (or at new employee induction), those employees will develop meaningful roles and connect with the mission of the organization. They will reach high levels of engagement within their first year as they figure out how best to contribute to organizational success.

We see a dip in engagement levels in years two through four, and a rise in engagement in subsequent years. This early drop-off in engagement is a reason for concern especially because research suggests that it will take an employee 8 to 28 weeks to hit high levels of productivity in most positions.

This bathtub curve may lead us to a simple conclusion: to reach high engagement levels, employees should give new jobs a chance—and stick with them. Job-hopping too early means you miss the chance to engage.

But the reality is quite different and is a lesson in engagement drivers. Some employees develop strong expertise and focus in the same role over several years. They find their positions fulfilling and enjoy the ability to contribute in these established roles.

Other employees are not as lucky and spend a number of years trying to find the work that's most satisfying for them.

In a work environment where the average tenure with a given employer is 4.4 years,[13] having 5 or more years of experience to develop expertise in a given role may seem like a luxury. The world of work in the 21st century is far more mobile, with its many voluntary departures, untimely promotions, and workforce downsizing.

A key takeaway from this dynamic is that organizations need to pay particular attention to designing employees' next roles and timing future transitions. The excitement and energy an employee may feel when moving into a promising new role may fade fast if the job turns out to be a poor fit. The topic of career is explored in depth in Chapter 9.

Is there an optimum shelf life for an individual employee in any given position? It depends on both the job and the individual, but research by the Institute for Corporate Productivity (i4cp) suggests that there is a point of diminishing returns. If an employee remains in the same role for more than 10 years, productivity falls.

In any engagement conversation, it will be important for the manager to discuss career and life cycle, and to pay attention to career outliers (those people new to a role, or people who remain in a role much longer than the average tenure for that position). This will all vary depending on a specific industry and dynamic of any organization.

For example, many organizations have identified the risk of employees leaving a given department. They plan specific initiatives to check in with employees around those milestones to ensure they remain committed. If the employees do not quit after the danger zone is passed, you can be sure they are staying for the right reasons.

Tony Ling, VP of human resources at Internet portal Dianping.com (China's largest restaurant review website), describes such a program to retain technical talent: "Zhang Tao [CEO] and I dedicate a lot of time to spend with staff. If you join Dianping, you will meet both of us within three months of joining. In addition, we are cognizant of the three-year itch," he says, referring to the common symptom of turnover at around the 36-month mark. So at around that time, senior leadership makes a point of personally reconnecting with staff.

These meetings are typically small-group lunches at which employees can challenge the CEO and the VP of human resources on any topic. "People are typically interested in issues of compensation, strategy, well-being and personal development," Ling says.

These are topics that he finds are directly correlated with why employees might leave at this stage and present an opportunity to reconnect them with the company's core mission and strategy.

Compare this to the approach at Big Blue: one executive at IBM China that we interviewed candidly admits,

> Turnover at the five year mark is healthy. . . . We like to bring in fresh blood and fresh perspectives. People recently hired are more excited, and after a while they get too comfortable.

IBM knows it has a strong employee brand in the country. Some young graduates are clearly attracted to IBM as a career stepping-stone.

"They are looking at adding the IBM brand to their resume, and to access specific [technical] resources," says the executive.

And so the firm attracts young and eager computer graduates or project managers and works them hard on projects for four or five years. When these employees eventually leave and move on to a competitor, executives do not fret nor do they feel betrayed.

While IBM's turnover is good in comparison to the rest of the industry, the firm is realistic about its chances of retaining top graduates in an overheated economy. Competitors will offer up to a 40 percent pay increase to attract IBM's employees.

"We do focus on the three-year review because that's a critical turning point," he says. "But if an employee has an attractive offer from a competitor, we won't usually try to match it financially. Our retention is very selective based on contribution and performance."

Some Industries See Higher
Engagement. But Who Cares?

As we look across industries, we understandably see variation in engagement levels as an aggregate. This may lead us to say that some industries are engaging and others are less so.

For example, a 2010 research report by Transparent Consulting studied the companies of the United Kingdom's FTSE-100 organized in 20 sectors. It concluded, "Companies and sectors which prioritize customer satisfaction are also the ones that seem to find it worthwhile to give attention to employee engagement."[14]

The report listed that the highest-rated sectors are Banks (score of 69), Insurance, Utilities, Telecommunications, and Media. The lowest levels of customer satisfaction according to the scale were Food and Beverages, Technology, Industrial General, Household, Leisure, and Personal Goods. Mining scored a lowly 30 (the lowest ranked sector).

This would appear to make sense; industries where there is a more immediate, tangible connection between employee engagement and customer attraction/retention will be paying far more attention to an employee's engagement. But what meaning does this have for you?

The main thing you want to take away from an industry benchmark is this: Is there a competitive advantage to be achieved in *your* industry by focusing on employee engagement? There are two answers:

1. You are operating in an industry where high engagement is the norm. If you are not able to engage your employees to the same degree, your organization will rapidly develop a reputation for not caring about employees or having a poorly defined strategy. You will suffer.

2. You operate in an industry where employee engagement is generally low. You have an opportunity to develop competitive advantage by outperforming competitors in your space by focusing on engagement. Online retailer Zappos is possibly the most well-known firm when it comes to building a successful company on a platform of employee (and consequently customer) engagement. Some of the company's practices, such as offering new hires $1,000 to quit if they do not feel that they belong, have become stuff of legend.[15]

How IndiGo Airlines Outperformed the Market

In 2011, India was among the world's fastest growing aviation markets, but its airline industry was losing billions of dollars. Then, through fuel price increases (70 percent higher than the global average), financial turmoil, and government action (airport tax hikes), any sign of growth virtually disappeared.

In late 2011, Kingfisher Airlines, then India's second-largest air carrier, reported record losses of $93 million, pushing its debt to $1.5 billion. The cash-strapped company had to cancel hundreds of flights and was late paying staff salaries. It rapidly dropped to last place in domestic airline rankings. Other large airlines operating in India experienced similar struggles.

But one airline was bucking the trend.[16]

IndiGo is a private, low-cost airline. While young, it is still the country's second-largest and the only airline in India currently making profit. The airline has grown faster than any other low-cost carrier in the world.

IndiGo is owned by the transportation group Interglobe Technologies (itself a top-50 Great Place to Work 2011 recipient, receiving the top spot as the Best Company in the Transportation Industry and second in the Best Recruitment, Selection, and Induction Category).[17] In 2011, IndiGo is known to have placed the largest order in commercial aviation history when Airbus won the $15 billion deal for 180 aircraft. By early 2012, IndiGo had taken the delivery of its 50th aircraft in less than six years.

So What's the Secret to IndiGo's Success?

It's IndiGo's business model: IndiGo's strong adherence to the low-cost model, buying only one type of plane, and keeping operational costs as low as possible. There's also heavy emphasis on on-time departures.

But part of IndiGo's business model is also a purposeful focus on employee engagement.

"Historically [in India], airlines did not feature in any of the best places to work–type lists. Aviation simply was not known for engagement or elaborate people practices. To us this was both an opportunity and a challenge. How do we restore the glamor and excitement of working for an airline?" says K.S. Bakshi, IndiGo's VP of human resources. "For young people especially, it is not seen as a long term career, aviation has been looked at as a 'career-less' industry, with a poor working environment."

Executives Who Jump

One final note on industries: many executives now jump between industries. Management skills often transfer effectively between sectors, but leadership is always contextual. Beware of bringing leaders from industries where employee engagement is not a priority into industries highly dependent on employee engagement.

Gender

We find that gender is not a significant factor when examining an employee population in most developed Western countries. On the other hand, in countries such as India or China, there is a noticeable gap (11 and 9 points, respectively) between men and women (with men being more engaged).

Overall, India still faces a large gap in education between boys and girls. Male literacy rates are 223 percent higher than those for females. A similar divide exists between genders in labor force participation rate and graduation rates by discipline. These broader gender differences are also reflected in company environments.

In China, gender inequality in the workplace is prevalent. The Chinese government admits "gender discrimination in employment is increasingly obvious" and is trying to address the issue.[18] Still, the ratio of average income between women and men progresses from 68 percent with a junior high school diploma, to 83 percent for college education. So while higher education may narrow the gap, women are still significantly underpaid when compared to their male counterparts.

Similar regional or country-specific dynamics will be at play wherever your organization is based. These are factors that outside the walls of your organization, are out of your control. But these factors present an opportunity to build a culture that is truly inclusive. Employees in these regions may place a much higher value on an employer that walks the talk on inclusiveness compared to employees in Europe or the United States, where the gender gap, while still present, is arguably not as acute.

Baxter is an example of an employer that stands out for bucking the gender gap. The pharmaceutical firm has been recognized for its diversity efforts. It has set high expectations, including a 50/50 gender split in senior leadership roles.

"There are many studies that show the benefits of gender diversity in leadership," says one of their executives in China. "In the China team we have 75 percent of women on the executive team."

The greater the social inequality between genders, the greater the opportunity for the organization to use this as a lever of engagement for employees that are disfavored outside of the enterprise. This is true for gender and other criteria of social discrimination and has been the case made by human resource professionals working in the area of diversity.

Unions Get a Bad Rap

Maybe it is the painful experience of negotiating with union leaders (and the sometimes acrimonious relationships that result), but most executives dealing with a unionized workforce start with the assumption that union workers are less engaged. This is not the case.

If unions had a significant impact on employee engagement, we would see higher support for unions, increased membership, and a growing trend of workers attracted to unionized environments. But trends are moving in the opposite direction.

In the United States, union membership is at a 25-year low: 12.4 percent of workers were union members in 2008.[19] Along with a decline in membership, we have observed a decline in popular support for unionization. Only 48 percent of the general population approves of labor unions.[20]

While workers may turn to unionization to address collective grievances, unionization itself has little impact on personal engagement. Nor does unionization have a strong positive or negative correlation with productivity.

According to the research group Gallup, "The difference in performance between union and non-union groups is minimal (approximately 6 percent). But engagement does create dramatic differences in productivity. Compared to the median, highly engaged workgroups (those at the 90th percentile) have, on average, 32.8 percent higher productivity."[21] This is regardless of whether the workgroup is unionized or not.

The one noteworthy connection between union membership and engagement may be this: most individuals have a strong need to belong to a group, a community with a larger purpose. This partially explains the explosive growth of Internet-based social media. Yet unions have declined as a platform for social unity. In the United Kingdom, working men's clubs (the social heart of the unionized working class) are shutting down at a rate of two per month.[22] Today, we see many savvy organizations build environments and cultures where these social needs are met in the workplace, not through labor movements or workers associations. These needs are met through company-sponsored initiatives.

So the decline of unions around the world opens an opportunity for companies to engage their workers by providing the sense of community and social fabric that is eroding elsewhere. Arguably, this was the initial momentum behind corporate interest in employee engagement. Organizations that excel at this will see long-term disinterest in union membership among their employees.

K. Ramkumar, executive director of ICICI Bank (India's largest private bank), says the bank has avoided union action despite acquiring numerous banks with high union representation.

ICICI has virtually no union membership. "In our experience, unionization is the result of abusive management," says

Ramkumar. "ICICI has always steered clear of political affiliation or union affiliation. We are very blunt about it. We believe that effective leadership starts with treating a human being as a human being—the day we stop abiding by that principal, unions will emerge. We believe the best protection from hostile union activity is to have a work culture where people can speak up without the fear of reprisal, threat, swearing, or transfer."

Takeaways

- If we look at engagement across industries and geographies, we see some interesting high-level trends.
- From these macro-observations, we offer some general guidelines that you can take back to your organization.

Shared Accountability and Daily Priority

The last chapter's trends and insights may be interesting, but the question remains: How can you increase engagement in *your own* organization?

There's a scenario unfolding in organizations around the world year after year. It goes something like this:

> The executive team decides that employee engagement needs to be part of the organization's ongoing strategy. They instinctively turn to the HR chief, who in turn consults some external "experts." Together they agree that they should start with a survey to gather some preliminary data and do some benchmarking against competitors.

A core team (made up entirely of HR staff) works with the external firm, agonizing over the questions to ask and demographic details that will shape the analysis.

The company has great expectations for the survey. Data is sliced and diced for weeks, or maybe even months, of analysis. Reports are generated that identify areas of opportunity and strengths.

Meetings are held where 80-slide presentations communicate the survey findings. Executives challenge the process or explain away disappointing numbers ("Not bad in light of the recession" or "Well, we have reorganized the department since then").

Organization-wide priorities are identified and task forces are created. Cascading communications reveal the highlights and the action plans. Managers are informed that they now own these action plans and are expected to increase their team's numbers by the next survey.

And things go dark. Managers go back to running the business, and they hear little, if anything, from senior leadership on the topic of engagement. Individuals on their teams go on—unaware.

Months later, as the next survey approaches, HR rattles a few cages, and asks, "Where are you going with your action plans?" Task forces reassemble and action plans suddenly get dusted off. A few programs are hastily implemented in time (one hopes) to boost the scores of the next survey. Employees are again asked for input because it is now that time of the year when everybody's opinion counts!

In the meantime, the executive team is looking to the head of HR, asking why this engagement thing hasn't happened yet.

For organizations that let a survey cycle drive the process, engagement becomes a once-a-year burst of activity, instead of a year-round responsibility. Initiatives are boiled down to a slap on the wrist and a list of to-dos. Managers often feel ill-equipped to undertake the actions, and the next survey seems a long way down the road. There are plenty of other day-to-day priorities and typically the thinking is, "This engagement thing can wait."

Surveys themselves don't accomplish anything. They are useful tools that have their place in informing and sustaining engagement efforts. But the cycle of surveying, analyzing data, communicating findings, and action planning has not served most organizations well.

Instead, we would like to propose an alternative—a holistic view of engagement across the enterprise that occurs not annually but on a daily basis. It's one that takes place not as an aside to the work but as the actual way the work gets done. It is not owned by HR or dumped on unsuspecting and ill-equipped managers but is a shared responsibility at all levels.

Before we get to this view of engagement, let's quickly summarize why most engagement initiatives falter.

Why Most Engagement Initiatives Fall Short

We've already emphasized one of your biggest challenges: engagement is fundamentally an individualized equation. The factors that influence it, especially the core drivers of satisfaction, vary from one individual to the next. That means there are limits to what broad-brush initiatives can accomplish.

Another problem is *ownership*. When you delegate engagement to your human resources department, unit leaders, or an ad hoc team, the rest of your organization thinks the issue is resolved. They believe that engagement is not *their* job. We have seen this failure with innovation efforts. When an innovation department is created, frontline employees (who have the most insight on ways to do their jobs better) abdicate all responsibility for improvements.

And finally, most action planning just doesn't deliver. We see three main reasons for this:

1. *Going through the motions of compliance:* If your workforce is like many, the first response to organizational action-planning mandates is to ignore the hoopla in hopes that it will go away (as most initiatives do). If energy remains high among senior leadership, harried managers then size up the consequences of noncompliance and go through the motions of action planning. Often this involves an online tracking system filled with half-hearted ideas that perhaps someday they'll pursue. (Stop here for a moment: Does this sound at all like your annual performance management process? That is fodder for another book.)

2. *Committed to the process, but fighting too many fires:* If you're convinced that your workforce is not faking compliance, and all your leaders and employees are well-intentioned and enthused about engagement, realize this—the more important work always rises to the top. Action plans, which are rarely seen as more important, are shelved in the face of new, urgent mandates, important client projects, unexpected problems, the ripple effects of budget cuts, and all the other priorities of doing business as usual.

3. *Action plans with no authority:* Some managers and task forces take their action plans to heart, but focus on items beyond their scope of influence or authority. Disappointed by the rejection when they propose some wide-reaching initiative, they run out of steam.

Do Not Separate Engagement
from the Work to Be Done

The trick, then, is to make engagement a *daily priority*. In the most successful organizations, engagement and results are discussed regularly—in the same breath.

As Matthew Froggatt, chief development officer at TNS (a market research firm, part of advertising giant WPP), says,

> The mindset has to shift away from *"today I am doing the employee commitment stuff."* Management is not a "mode" nor do you have "management days" of the week. These things only live and breathe in organizations when people instinctively see it as part of their job—to sense and respond, to have emotional intelligence, to be aware of how people are feeling.

Engagement is not a flavor of the month or once-a-year initiative. It's something leaders worry about every day because engagement is about getting work done. It is not about calling a time-out to get people engaged by spinning their plate, and then getting back to work, hoping the energy that keeps them aloft does not peter out too soon.

Everyone Owns a Piece of
the Engagement Equation

If engagement is to become a daily priority, it has to be a shared responsibility. Leaders and managers cannot and should not shoulder the entire burden of engaging your workforce. Every member needs to play a role (or several roles), as individuals (I), managers (M), or executives (E).

Individuals

Since employees approach their work from a wide variety of personal situations and with a unique blend of values, talents, interests, and ambitions, they must ultimately be responsible for their own engagement. They are at the heart of the engagement model introduced in Chapter 1 as they pursue their personal definition of success while delivering what your organization needs. If they don't know what they want, hate their work, or make bad career moves, they can't expect their manager or your organization to fix it.

Managers

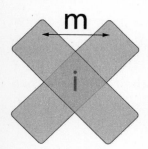

For our purposes, the term *managers* refers to employees' immediate supervisors—regardless of their title or level in the hierarchy. By their very role, managers are in a position to align employee and organizational interests, as represented in the model here. They should know what the organization needs and what their individual team members can and want to do. Managers already understand that their job is to accomplish results through others (setting expectations and coaching employees toward maximum contribution). They need to balance out both sides of the equation by also understand individual satisfaction drivers.

And since managers are individuals first, *they need to take control of their own engagement.*

Executives

We are defining executives as senior managers who are two or more steps removed from individuals, have a broad scope of accountability, and hold visible senior leadership positions (e.g., plant managers, department heads, or senior team members). These leaders set the overall tone and 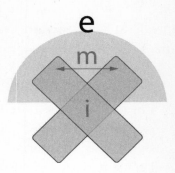 culture of the organization (illustrated by the half-moon shadow behind the X in the model here). While they are responsible for crafting and clearly communicating the organization's definition of success, they should not be involved in the day-to-day individual alignment of interests, talents, and priorities (unless it's for their direct reports).

Executives, like managers and individuals, still need to manage their own engagement.

The Organization

While not a segment of the workforce, organizational practices and policies (e.g., rewards and recognition, performance management) can have wide-reaching effects on engagement levels. Typically executives and/or human resources leaders shape these practices and must ensure that they do not run counter to engagement efforts.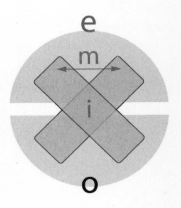

This 3+1 structure of ownership, which we refer to as IME/O, helps ensure that one type of engagement lever is not undermining progress made elsewhere. For the rest of this chapter, we will examine the roles and responsibilities of IME—the *people* in your workforce. We will explore organizational practices (O) in the discussion of culture in Chapter 6.

> Engagement is not just an organizational issue. It's a managerial issue, so the behavior of managers is critical. But it's also an individual issue, in terms of understanding "my" engagement—why I come to work and what engages me with the organization and the role that I fulfill. I think if you ignore any one of those levels, you miss being able to understand the impact properly.
> —*David Spicer, senior lecturer in organizational change and head of the Human Resources Management group at Bradford University School of Management in the United Kingdom*

Individuals Need to ACT

Well-managed organizations define, refine, communicate, and focus resources toward clear definitions of success. But what about employees? It's rare to find individuals who are crystal clear on what they want out of life. Many people know it when they find it, but when they're not achieving high satisfaction, they struggle to determine why they are unfulfilled. Others think they know what fulfills them, but discover once they attain their goals, that they were chasing after the wrong things.

If employees are not clear on their core values and goals—and the talents that power their contribution—they will not become engaged in your workplace (or potentially any other). You need to help them gain clarity on their engagement drivers, understand what the organization requires, and empower them to make the changes necessary to reach full engagement.

We use the acronym ACT (Assess, Communicate, Take action) to describe the responsibilities.

A = Assess personal values, interests, talents, and goals—as well as their understanding of the organization's priorities.

C = Communicate to share what is important to them—and to better understand what the organization needs.

T = Take action.

Goals Are a Moving Target

Much has been written about a study on personal objectives involving the Harvard class of 1979, popularized in the book *What They Don't Teach You in the Harvard Business School*, by Mark McCormack. According to the study, those students who were crystal clear on their own objectives, in the form of a written set of personal goals, went on to earn significantly more than those who did not. This study (and another variant that featured Yale graduates) turns out to be fiction.[1]

That's okay with us, because we made the case in Chapter 1 that money isn't everything. More importantly, general, long-term aspirations in today's world of work will serve most employees better than tightly defined ambitions. Our reasoning? The pace of change is far too quick. Yesterday's goals reflect yesterday's jobs and opportunities. Instead, your employees need to have a sense of where they want to go and why, and then regularly assess and reevaluate those goals. (The challenge of today's constantly changing career landscape is explored in Chapter 9.)

Consequently, to equip individuals for success, you should focus not on action planning and discrete objectives, but on providing a framework that will help them individually determine what will meet their unique definition of satisfaction. This will allow them to take ownership of their current engagement and navigate future opportunities, no matter how unforeseen. To quote then-general Dwight D. Eisenhower, "Plans are useless, but planning is indispensable."

The Value of Values

In Chapter 1 we made the point that job fit—a combination of meaningful work and suitable job conditions—is a key engagement driver and that personal values strongly influence that fit. BlessingWhite's 40 years of values clarification work with over a million people worldwide indicates that people usually have an immediate response to the question, What are your top five values? Yet after a series of exercises, the vast majority redefine their list by adding values and deleting others. To make matters more complicated, intangible terms like *achievement*, *integrity*, or *family happiness* are subject to individual interpretation, so even when your team shares a particular value, how it plays out for them on the job may differ.

Values also influence emotional commitment to your organization. Barry Posner and Warren Schmidt's 1992 study indicated that employees who "had the greatest clarity about both personal and organizational values had the highest degree of commitment to the organization."[2] No matter how clear you may be in communicating your organization's values, the implication is that if employees aren't aware of their personal motivators, they won't be willing to engage fully and contribute to the organization's goals. As Posner points out (with Jim Kouzes) in *The Leadership Challenge*, "Those individuals with the clearest personal values are better prepared to make choices based on principle—including deciding whether the principles of the organization fit with their own personal principles."[3]

Talents + Work Priorities = Contribution

To achieve full engagement, employees need to understand their strengths and weaknesses so they can focus their talents effectively. Of course, to effectively focus, they need to understand what the organization needs from them—and why. These aspects of engagement are typically addressed in performance management processes and are areas where managers (in theory) play a role with goal setting, feedback, and development.

Accountability to Communicate and Act

The inadequacies of systems and managers in driving performance means that individuals need to move from a passive "Tell me what to do and how I'm doing" mode to a proactive one. Ideally, employees should not wait for a tap on the shoulder to signal a career move or exciting new project. They need to take initiative to build their skill sets, articulate their interests, satisfy their core values, and identify ways to apply their talents to achieve your organization's goals. They need to initiate conversations about reshaping their jobs, clarifying their work priorities, or getting the support they need from their managers.

ACTing on Your Engagement: Best Practice for Individuals

Assess the Variables That Shape Maximum Satisfaction

- *Clarify your personal values.* There are a number of approaches you can use, but the most important step is to filter out any *should* values and identify the top five

(Continued)

that are truest to you. Then, in your own words, take the extra step of defining what each value means to you.

- *Identify your strengths.* Draw up a crisp list of your core strengths but don't rely only on self-assessment. Ask for feedback from colleagues or your manager about what you do best.

- *Consider your interests and long-term goals.* You don't need a specific game plan, but it helps to understand which skills you would like to develop or what work experiences you'd like to gain.

- *Determine your preferred job conditions.* Under what conditions do you do your best work? Minimal or high supervision? Structured or free-wheeling approaches? Flexible hours? Collaborative or solo projects?

Assess Your Understanding of Maximum Contribution

Consider the following aspects of your job. Your responses are not necessarily the correct answers. You'll need to talk with your manager (as part of the two-way dialogue we describe below).

- *Your job's connection to the organization's strategy and mission.* What would happen if your role did not exist? Who benefits from the work that you do?

- *Your top three work priorities.* What are the most important results that you need to accomplish in the next one to three months?

- *Skills required for success.* What skills are most important to accomplishing your priorities?

- *Requirements for how the work must be done.* What expectations does your manager have for the conditions under which you work? How does he like to work?

- *Your manager's priorities.* What are your manager's challenges and goals? They also shape yours.

Communicate: Start a Two-Way Dialogue

- *Compare and confirm your understanding of your job with your manager.* Do this even if you think you are on the same page with your manager about expectations, priorities, required skills, and job conditions. We guarantee you'll uncover disconnects. If your job has changed recently or your manager is new, there will be a lot of gaps in how both of you perceive your role.

- *Talk about ways to leverage your strengths.* Using your talents more will increase your satisfaction *and* contribution.

- *Discuss aspects of your job that you would like to change or maintain.* Don't overlook discussing the conditions you enjoy. If your manager doesn't know that these conditions increase your satisfaction, she may eliminate them.

- *Brainstorm development ideas* for ensuring you have the skills required for current success *and* for satisfying your long-term aspirations.

- *Discuss how to best work together.* Do this even if you've known your manager for years. Pay particular attention to decision making and communications, and make sure to ask about any pet peeves.

(Continued)

- *Gain commitment.* If your agreed plan of action gets shelved when the next crisis or big project hits, you will make little progress. Commit to your actions, and make sure your manager commits to supporting you in your plan.

Taking Action

- *Act on the things that you can influence or control.*
- *Identify how you can change your own behavior* to better satisfy your values. What can you start, stop, or continue doing today?
- *Decide to be more engaged.* Do not dismiss this point. According to human potential expert Shawn Achor (*The Happiness Advantage*), "happiness and optimism actually *fuel* performance." Shift your mindset to be engaged in spite of any negativity around you or a challenging business environment.
- *Don't attempt to fix every weakness.* Work on those that interfere with current success in your job or threaten your career aspirations.
- *Find ways to stay the course.* Whether it is keeping a journal, regular check-ins with your manager to discuss progress, or finding a friend to act as a coach, find some approach you are comfortable with to establish milestones and maintain momentum.

By working together, employees and their immediate managers can work as a team to achieve an outcome that is in the best interest of both parties. Naturally, managers need to be receptive to those conversations and coach effectively, which brings us to the next role in the equation: the M.

Influencing the I

As a leader, what's in your control?

- Set expectations of employee ownership for personal and professional success.
- Hire and promote employees who demonstrate initiative.
- Provide training and tools to help employees gain clarity and act on their personal drivers, goals, and talents.
- Be crystal clear in your communications about strategy so that the messages translated into employees' daily priorities are also crystal clear.

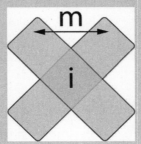

Managers Need to CARE about Engagement

The general trend in organizations is toward leaner, flatter, and more matrix-based structures. At the same time, the pace of change, innovation, and volume of communications are all growing. As a result, managers are caught between a rock and a hard place: more fluid, ambiguous, and fast-paced work environments and, as player-coaches, less time to spend on the spinning plates we likened employees to in the Preface.

So what do most organizations do? Place the burden of employee engagement solely on the managers' shoulders, with results that are patchy at best. That's because managers cannot *make* employees engaged; they can only *facilitate* their team members' engagement journeys. To help managers understand how they can drive engagement daily (as opposed to a once-a-year survey-driven activity), we use the acronym CARE—Coach, Align, Recognize, and Engage.

> C = Coach individuals toward maximum contribution *and* satisfaction.
>
> A = Align and constantly re-align individuals to the organization's strategy, mission, and values.
>
> R = Recognize attitude, effort, and results.
>
> E = Engage in dialogue about what's important to both parties, *while at the same time* engaging themselves.

Relationships as a Foundation

The more employees feel they know their managers, the more engaged they are likely to be. In some regions of the world, this factor is even more important than effectiveness of coaching and leadership skills.[4] Rodney Miller, former dean of the corporate university for FPL, a U.S.-based utility, has seen the impact firsthand:

> Coaching is one of the most important leadership behaviors. It hinges on the relationship, the employees' trust, and the belief that the manager has their best interests at heart.

This is an important caveat to the CARE model. Managers must drop the veil of their position or title, and become better known to employees. That doesn't necessarily mean being their buddy. But it does mean sharing personal motivation for work, challenges, appropriate weaknesses, the reasons they came to your organization, and why they stay there. (We discuss ways to do this in Chapter 8.)

The Coaching Conundrum

When we talk about coaching for engagement, managers need to

- Understand each team member's unique interests, talents, and aspirations.
- Assign tasks that marry individuals' passion and proficiencies with organizational priorities and projects.
- Provide development opportunities to build talents.
- Keep the dialogue going, providing feedback and course corrections to ensure maximum satisfaction and contribution.

This expectation is reasonable since coaching is part of what managers are supposed to do to get results. Unfortunately, although most managers believe in coaching and like to coach, they don't do it. Time constraints are often blamed, as is a lack of formal coaching skills. In addition, few organizations actually hold managers accountable or tie compensation to coaching their people.[5]

The leadership transition of first-time managers is often challenging. Newly-promoted managers do not typically adjust quickly to the balance of their new roles: they focus on task completion instead of people development.

This situation may be one of the biggest stumbling blocks to creating a more engaged workforce. It underscores our point of view that low engagement levels are not caused by badly behaved managers, but by managers not being clear on their accountabilities or not seizing the opportunities they have to coach their teams to higher levels.

A Never-Ending Alignment Story

Engagement is a case of give and take—of gaining satisfaction and giving contribution. Once engagement has been achieved, there are many factors that may cause it to get out of balance, one being the constant shifting and redirecting of organizational strategy and direction. As each department or team changes tack, it is up to the manager to ensure that employees make course corrections to stay aligned with the most immediate priorities.

If left alone, individuals may also be tempted to chase satisfaction at the expense of contribution. Even the best-intentioned employees understand that their relationship with the organization comes with few guarantees. A project that will look great on a resume might be favored over less satisfying work that is critical to the organization.

It is the manager's role to address this balance, aligning daily priorities to meet the outputs required by the organization. This type of alignment is part of routine coaching, but as we described previously, it can't be taken for granted. Chapter 7 explores the challenges and best practices of alignment of strategy organization-wide.

The Art of Recognition

Most research identifies recognition as a driver of engagement, and as a consequence, many companies adopt some form of enterprise-wide online platform. This platform attempts to formalize the recognition process, generate organization-wide metrics, and encourage the use of recognition within teams and across departments.

It's a noble attempt that suffers from two shortfalls.

First, formal recognition and rewards programs are often disconnected from the strategy. Managers are unclear about when and why to use the recognition process, what the nomination process is (if any), or their ability and scope to use discretionary rewards. In the absence of clear cues, recognition becomes erratic, with some managers using it at every opportunity while others snub the process entirely.

Next, corporate-sponsored initiatives can come across as inauthentic or less sincere than a personal gesture.

Managers who skillfully use recognition to drive engagement do not rely on corporate programs. They understand that praise and acknowledgment are sometimes valued more than movie tickets or an acrylic paperweight. Ultimately, recognition is more art than science.

- Managers zero in on behaviors they wish to see replicated again and again.
- They understand their team members and know each one's strengths—and limitations.
- They set individual expectations and recognize those team members who distinguish themselves through their efforts.

As with most engagement factors, recognition is a personal preference—it takes a skilled manager to know what form of recognition or reward will be most meaningful to each individual. If in doubt, the best approach is to simply ask each person.

Alain Moffroid of Unilever puts it this way: "The most disengaged people at Unilever had bosses that didn't take the time. A simple phone call can make all the difference. It's about how managers make you feel about yourself. Ultimately, it's about how you feel about yourself in your job."

Engagement at Two Levels

When we say that managers need to engage, we're talking about two different things:

1. They must take control of their own engagement.
2. They must engage each individual on the team in regular conversations about what matters most to both parties.

Managers must first fulfill the responsibilities of individual employees described earlier in this chapter, because disengaged managers cannot help employees become more engaged, much in the same way that a lost ship captain cannot guide his crew to get back on course. Every day, they need to monitor and take control of their own engagement. (Chapter 5 contains tips on how to do this.)

Managers must also engage in dialogue. These regular conversations are such an important element of the engagement equation that we devote Chapter 8 to them.

Equipping the M

As a leader, how do you ensure that your managers fuel engagement in others?

- Set expectations and hold managers accountable for results *and* engagement.
- Hire and promote managers with proven people skills.
- Train managers to be effective coaches.
- Reinforce strategy so that the messages translated into employees' daily priorities are clear. (A Hamster boss will lead her team into Hamster territory.)

- Remove barriers to people management by being realistic about the effectiveness of player-coaches and managers with large spans of control.
- Reinforce a culture of dialogue and engagement as a daily priority.

Executives Need to Build a CASE for Engagement

As an executive, you are not in the position to coach and align the personal interests of each and every employee. Yet as Andrew Reeves, CEO of George Weston Foods, cautions, your role is critical:

> Many leaders underestimate the impact they can have on people. Everything you do as a leader sends a message about what you value and what you focus on.

You must set the direction that your workforce aligns to, communicate that direction to ensure a clear line of sight throughout your organization, and create a culture that fuels engagement *and* business results. You must also fulfill the role of manager and individual as previously described. We understand that this is a tall order.

We need to look at the priorities of executives in leading a workforce to higher engagement from the perspective of the leaders' followers. Our focus therefore is not on the intrinsic qualities that may make you an effective leader but instead is about asking, "What are the needs of followers that I as a leader need to fulfill?" We find it useful to talk about how you build your CASE (Community, Authenticity, Significance, and Excitement).

These are core needs of the 21st century workforce (your followers) and are useful in delivering results as well as engagement.[6]

C = Community for a sense of belonging and purpose
A = Authenticity as a basis for trust and inspiration
S = Significance to recognize individuals' contributions
E = Excitement to constantly encourage—and raise the bar on—high performance

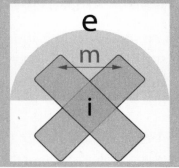

Community

The emotional commitment associated with engagement will result, in part, from employees connecting to each other, and to the organization. Gareth Jones and Rob Goffee of the London Business School described it this way in their book *Why Should Anyone Be Led by You?*:

> Human beings are hard-wired for sociability and desire solidarity. They have a deep-rooted desire to belong, to feel part of something bigger, to relate to others—not just the leader.[7]

This means that executives need to foster a community in which employees can belong and actively participate. Mark Hales, director of mission at St Vincents & Mater Health, a medical center in Sydney, Australia, describes how his organization builds community around the heritage and values of the founding sisters and helps connect people to what matters most in their lives—their work and, most importantly, their relationships. Hales sums up these needs:

> In society we used to find and experience community in our extended families, neighborhoods, community groups and our churches. Today we live more isolated lives and the most social interaction we might find is at the mall on Saturdays. We only know our neighbors in our apartment block exist because the lights go on and off. So we understand the importance of finding meaningful community at work. We do a lot to connect our staff and make them feel how we—both individually and collectively—make a difference. How work, and the experience of being together making a difference, is something that gives us meaning and purpose.

Community and belonging do not have to have a purpose as mission-driven as St Vincents, as long as you can help employees answer "Why are we here?" and "What can we achieve together?"

One organization that elevated its sense of purpose is India's Oil and Natural Gas Corporation (ONGC Ltd.), a state-owned company involved in finding and exploiting hydrocarbons. ONGC is one of Asia's largest oil and gas exploration and extraction companies, with 77 percent of India's crude oil production (and 30 percent of total domestic demand). It also produces 81 percent of India's natural gas.

"India won't be energy independent anytime soon," says K S Jamestin, director of human resources, pointing out that India only produces enough oil to account for 20 percent of domestic consumption, whereas energy demand is growing at a steady 6 to 8 percent per year.

This provides ONGC with a strong sense of mission: to reduce India's reliance on foreign energy. To accomplish this, ONGC's engineers are working in the "frontier areas" of exploration—the unexplored wilderness and the deepest parts of the ocean.

"Our employees need to have a strong sense of adventure," says Jamestin. "But we are also aware of the challenges of being out in the field. Our best performers can suffer from burn-out." The inspirational goal of helping the country increase energy independence helps keep the organization focused and the workforce engaged in this challenging undertaking.

Authenticity and Trust

Followers look to authentic leaders for inspiration. Yet many senior leaders attempt to emulate the leadership style of others rather than discover their own authentic voice. Followers respond to connection skills, not just pure business competence. They seek out leaders who are different in meaningful ways, but are not pretending to be perfect. Effective leaders learn to skillfully leverage both their strengths and weaknesses when engaging with their followers.

Followers look for credible leaders who appear genuine and trustworthy. Indeed, most engagement studies demonstrate a correlation between trust in leadership and high engagement, sending a clear mandate that executives must build trust. The challenge for leaders at the top is that they don't have to make sensational headlines or land in jail to be perceived as less than trustworthy.

Executives suffer from high visibility and low interactivity. Unlike employees' immediate managers, who can demonstrate their trustworthiness through daily employee-manager interactions, executives must earn the trust of employees they see occasionally or may never meet in person.

Less engaged employees can be quick to speculate and make negative assessments on why decisions were made or actions taken. Engaged employees are less cynical. They understand what needs to be done and care enough to apply discretionary effort. So for them especially, executive communications need to cover the *what* and *why* of decisions. In the same way students must show the math, explaining how they reach correct answers in algebra class, leaders need to share the business rationale and personal motivation for critical business decisions. Executive actions, too, need to demonstrate visible *personal commitment* to the success of the organization as a business venture and thriving workplace.

Aside from doing what you say you will do, communication is always the best tool for demonstrating the type of authenticity that inspires workforce commitment. Author and executive coach Terry Pearce calls this *communicating from the inside out*. "You must understand how to bring yourself authentically, in your real skin, to the full range of situations that will move your advocacy forward."[8]

Ultimately, it's the consistency of executive communications and executive actions that creates trust.

Significance

Effective leaders make their followers feel that their contribution is adding significant value to fulfilling the purpose of the enterprise. While this attribute has strong parallels with the recognition role of managers, there are some important distinctions.

Managers are working one-on-one with their team members, identifying specific contributions and reinforcing specific outcomes that are beneficial to the organization. For senior leaders, the task is to break through hierarchical, social, or cultural barriers and ensure that each individual feels that her contribution is valued. Whether it is in corporate communications, time dedicated to departmental reviews, or personalized hand-written notes, there are many channels available to senior leaders to reinforce the appreciation of individual contributions to the greater purpose.

The message is simple: "As a senior leader, I notice these contributions every day, they contribute to our success, and I thank you for them."

Excitement

Workplaces have an energy level. It may be high, or it may be low, but you can certainly feel it. Leaders establish the level of positive energy that flows through an office, a retail space, or a shop floor. We have seen workplaces positively buzzing with energy days after a visit by a senior leader.

Excitement comes in different flavors: it may be a quiet but tense level of energy in a research lab or the loud externalized excitement of a trading floor. It could be the laid-back-yet-intense vibe of a dot-com. But whatever the flavor, it is an energy that fuels people's focus and commitment to getting the job done.

Leaders can create excitement in several ways. It may be by sharing the mission and purpose of the enterprise in new and compelling ways. It may be personally connecting with individuals and just listening to their stories. It may be by challenging an underperforming team to bring up its game.

But primarily, it is about tapping into his own passions and engagement, and finding a compelling way to communicate this to followers. This is why a leader needs to be in the apex (see Figure 1.1) to truly excite others to exceptional performance.

Executing the E

As a leader, what do you need to do?

- You must take control of your own engagement before you can inspire the workforce to do the same. Read Chapter 5.
- Then read the chapters on culture building, strategy alignment, and dialogue.
- Build your CASE by infusing a sense of Community, Significance, and Excitement, while demonstrating your Authenticity as a leader.
- Hold yourself and your peers accountable for results *and* engagement.
- Take care in all that you say *and* do.

Takeaways

- Making engagement a survey-action-planning cycle will typically result in short bursts of unproductive activity.
- Action planning falls flat because of unclear ownership, competing priorities, and the complexity of addressing individualized engagement equations.
- Do not separate engagement from the daily work, or it will never be a priority.
- All individuals (at all levels of the workforce) need to be clear on their personal strengths, values, and work

(Continued)

preferences. They need to take accountability for their success and act on their own engagement drivers.

- Managers must facilitate individuals' engagement equations through coaching, alignment, recognition, and continuous dialogue.

- Executives need to meet the needs of their followers (CASE) and hold managers accountable for delivering on their piece of the equation.

5

A Dead Battery Can't Jump-Start Another

As noted in the last chapter, organizations can't *make* employees engaged. All employees have to accept the responsibility for their own engagement and manage their own engagement equation. Let's start with *you*. As a leader, *you* have to go first.

Why is this important? Changing an organization is hard work. You need to be fully aligned and internally fueled to succeed. You know it takes a lot of energy to infuse your team with a sense of purpose and urgency. And while drive and enthusiasm can be positively infectious, disengagement is contagious, too. You can't fake being engaged.

It's also important to avoid one very common pitfall of engagement initiatives: the temptation to bypass senior levels. Many executive teams delegate engagement down, making the managers (and the managers alone) accountable to engage the worker bees, as if the senior team were beyond such requirements. If you want your initiative to be truly embedded, start at the top and work your way down, modeling the behaviors at each step of the way, never taking engagement for granted.

Let's spend a minute to explore your own engagement before embarking on an expedition to engage the entire organization. One dead battery can't jump-start another. Your team and your organization deserve your full commitment.

Challenges at the Top

Being an executive has its perks. But the role is becoming increasingly demanding, complicated, and unforgiving. Executives face challenges they never did in the past: the prevalence of 24/7 business operations, the mobile office that never lets you disconnect, and the increasing number of stakeholders your business has to contend with. Remember how simple it was when all you had to worry about were shareholders?

The advent of social media and the cynicism engendered by the growing pay disparity between the shop floor and the C-suite have eroded the social status of executives. They operate under a microscope in front of a highly critical audience.

Still, it is on executives that shareholders and members of the board rely, not just to plan and execute the business strategy, but to lead the organization, bringing along key investors, the media, and all employees. The physical and emotional demands of executive jobs can be extraordinary.

A Propensity for Engagement

Despite these demands, as a senior executive, you are about twice as likely to be engaged as the rest of your workforce.[1] This isn't surprising because

- As a senior leader you have more control over your work environment and have the power to make changes to support your increased satisfaction.

- You are also part of (or at least closer to) decision making about direction and strategy, so you should not be disconnected or misaligned. That, in turn, helps drive your maximum contribution and satisfaction.

- Those who make it to the executive suite often demonstrate a propensity for higher engagement throughout their career: they are promoted because of higher contribution, and their passion for their work is reflected in higher satisfaction.

However, 1 executive in 10 is likely to be among the Disengaged, and another four are likely to find themselves in one of the middle levels described in Chapter 2: Almost Engaged, Crash & Burners, or Honeymooners & Hamsters.

As a senior leader, you can most likely recall experiencing periods of less-than-full engagement like these throughout the course of your career:

- *This job is great but it isn't a fit now.* Your perspective on work can change as your personal priorities shift. Your definition of success may get reshaped, for instance, by changes in family situations or your health.

- *This isn't what you thought it would be!* You might have pursued opportunities that appeared to fit external definitions of success but that turn out to be unfulfilling. For example, to move up the chain of command, you took on responsibilities that do not energize you, and you delegate many of the tasks that once gave you a sense of personal achievement. This is a common symptom described by company founders who thrive in the early years of rapid growth only to feel burdened by the responsibility of running a larger organization. (See the sidebar later in this chapter for what Twitter co-founder and CEO Evan Williams did.)

- *Where's the bus going?* Shifts in organizational strategy and direction can leave you misaligned and uncertain about your commitment to the new focus.

- *Going through the motions.* This is perhaps the most troubling scenario—of quiet desperation that executive coach Terry Pearce says he often encounters. Pearce, the author of *Leading Out Loud,* works with senior executives on leadership communication and effectiveness. He warns, "Many executives who are not engaged *don't even know* that that they're not engaged. They're not aware of how good it can be."

- *Interpersonal conflicts will happen.* As the composition of the senior team changes, you will likely encounter peers with whom you don't see eye-to-eye. Locking horns with other senior leaders or poor team dynamics can cause disengagement.

The Role of Purpose

One particularly salient challenge at the executive level is *the role of purpose*. According to executive coach Paul Mitchell, the difference between those who can sustain the stress of executive roles and those who can't is how the significance of work and personal contribution are perceived—by themselves or by their peers. He explains, "If they feel that they are making a contribution, that what they do counts, they are able to operate at a very high level. The difference between those who succeed and those who burn out is whether or not they still believe in what they are doing."

"For an executive, this quest for meaning is what will sustain you; you have to be able to get up every morning with a sense that you can both *savor* and *save* the world," Mitchell continues. "Now executives can certainly savor the world—they are very well compensated and enjoy all that money can buy. But they also need to have a sense that they are *saving* the world, that they—or their business—are making a difference. It may not be saving humanity, but maybe the sense that they as an executive are making a difference to the people in the organization, through coaching or mentoring, or helping others develop their own path to success."

When Executives Spin Out of Control. . .

One way or the other, no one is immune to waking up one day and realizing that she has drifted out of the apex of the engagement model: lost, seemingly without enthusiasm, searching for meaning, or feeling that her contribution has been diminished.

As soon as a senior executive's energy goes, he will start to drift. If the CEO falls into despair, then the CEO's immediate team goes into despair, and eventually the whole organization follows. As the old saying goes, "A fish rots from the head down."

Take crashing and burning executives, for example. For years, they have given a tremendous amount. They may have sacrificed in their personal lives, withdrawn from their families, become physically exhausted, or suffered from stress-related health challenges. Their marriages may have fallen apart, and they may feel estranged from their children. Often, even if they feel able or willing to talk about these challenges, they have nobody to turn to.

"They often try to 'numb' themselves, if you like. They turn to food, alcohol, or work, and can become increasingly isolated socially," says Mitchell.

When spiraling toward disengagement, they may not recognize their own behavior—unless they have somebody else giving them feedback. It is therefore important that, if you find yourself drifting, you either find a way to recommit or get out of the way.

Who Calls a Time-Out?

One of the challenges of executive disengagement is the ability to expose and come to terms with the low state of engagement. Often in the senior ranks there is an expectation that people are functioning at a high level, and coaching conversations and engagement discussions occur less frequently.

And in the case of the CEO, there is no immediate boss to call a time-out.

Providing a Feedback Mechanism   Leadership at the top is a bubble. Despite having an open-door policy or making every effort to be approachable, your position creates a barrier to candor. People may not volunteer constructive feedback about your behavior. So you need to seek it out and then listen carefully instead of reacting to the observations shared.

Executives can get very isolated and do not always have a good feedback mechanism, so it is a good idea to have an early warning system. This should not be your spouse or partner; nobody wants to burden a loved one with these types of issues. An executive cannot easily bring this to her peers or the board of directors. So it helps to have a coach, a mentor (a senior executive in another company), or some kind of support network (a professional association of executives) who can provide frank and candid feedback. Find someone you can really open up to. There is something magical and cathartic in just stating where you are.

The reason executive coaching works so well is that in many cultures there is still a strong stigma about getting help, such as seeing a therapist. But an executive coach remains a bona fide external source of support and one that carries less of a stigma.

The Role of Boards in Addressing Low Executive Engagement
Since CEOs don't have the option of connecting with an immediate boss or even their peers, it falls to the board of directors to identify a CEO whose engagement has slipped. Many boards, however, fail to do so until it's too late, or they see the signs but decide to brush over them.

Board members need to look beyond short-term financial results and train themselves to pick up signs of disengagement—and to tackle it when they see it before the workforce and the bottom line suffer. Early warning signs include a lack of energy, fewer ideas being brought forward to the board, a less optimistic outlook, and more arguments during meetings.

Managing Your Own Engagement Equation

You should not need a survey or an executive coach to pinpoint your engagement level.

But beyond reaching out to others, you can just work on improving your self-awareness. Take time to slow down and reflect on where you are—and why. "The metaphor I use is that your activity creates ripples—which can interfere with reflection, just as they do in a pond. When the pond is calm, the ripples dissipate. Only then can you get a clear reflection of what is truly going on," Mitchell says. Pearce goes a step further with the executives he coaches, recommending technology-free days to "allow for space for ideas or insights to drop in."

Then you can identify what you can do to move into or stay in the apex of full engagement. Here are some important points to remember as you start to take control of your own engagement:

- *Engagement levels are never a given.* Individuals travel up and down on both the satisfaction and the contribution scales, depending on factors like those described in Chapter 1. A shift in organizational strategy can create misalignment, a string of difficult customer or colleague experiences can dampen enthusiasm and satisfaction. This means that you need to perform regular check-ups to identify which factors are putting your own engagement at risk.

- *Individuals need to ACT.* Chapter 4 provides detail on the responsibilities of all members of the workforce to own their personal engagement. You need to take initiative to develop self-awareness, articulate your interests, satisfy your core values, and identify ways to apply your talents so you can achieve the organization's goals. *And do this, of course, in parallel to your day job of leading others.*

If you are in doubt as to your ability to commit, here are some ideas as to where you might start.

Reflect

If you don't know what is important to you, you won't be able to find it in your current role—or any other job. This is a message you will read multiple times in this book because it is *that* important. Your personal definition of success must by crystal clear if you want to become more engaged. The Appendix contains additional exercises to bring clarity to your situation.

Start by considering these questions:

- Are you clear on your most important values, the things that give you joy, a sense of where you want to go, and the unique talents that you bring to the table?

- Are your values satisfied in your current role?
- Are your talents fully utilized?
- Why did you join the organization? Why do you stay? Are the reasons you joined still fueling you today?
- Which of the dozen things on your to-do list are your three mission-critical priorities?
  - Would *your boss* agree?
  - Would *your team* agree?
- What are you most proud of? (Hint: you're in trouble if you can't think of anything, or if you think survival is your proudest accomplishment.)

Continue by considering these questions, which are critical in assessing how engaged you are in the leadership role you need to play:

- Are you crystal clear on the company's strategy from high-level objectives down to tactics?
- How committed are you to making this future vision a reality?
- How passionate do you feel about getting others engaged in making this vision a reality?
- Are you committed to the long-term goals of the company, or are you looking at building a visible showcase for your next career step?

Ask for Feedback

Ask for impressions like these:

- Do you seem engaged to others?
- Where do people see you most energized?

- Are your personal motivators clear to those around you?
- Are your team members clear on their priorities? (If they're not, you may not be clear on yours.)

Take Action

What should you do when you have determined your own engagement level?

1. *Commit or quit.* You need to decide if you are ready for another year leading your company. If you feel bruised, make sure you are ready for another round in the boxing ring. If you are tired, recharge your battery. You cannot lead unless you are fully engaged. Your employees deserve more than a leader who is only half-in.

2. *Get out of your office and reconnect.* Talk to people inside and out to reignite your passion for your organization's mission. Remind yourself why your company is important. Talk to customers.

3. *Communicate the vision.* You need to create excitement and trust in your leadership. You should generate confidence in others that your company is on the right path. Communicating the vision will also help you stay personally connected.

How Evan Williams, Twitter Co-Founder and CEO, Managed His X

We refer to taking a proactive stance in aligning your strengths and passions to the needs of the organization as "managing your X" (referring to the X at the heart of our engagement model). In 2010, Evan Williams, CEO of Twitter, decided to step down—or rather step sideways. His explanation reflects the type of self-awareness required to sustain high levels of satisfaction and contribution. He wrote (italics are ours):

> The challenges of growing an organization so quickly are numerous. Growing big is not success, in itself. *Success to us means meeting our potential as a profitable company that can retain its culture and user focus while having a positive impact on the world.* This is no small task. I frequently reflect on the type of focus that is required from everyone at Twitter to get us there.
>
> This led to a realization as we launched the new Twitter. *I am most satisfied while pushing product direction. Building things is my passion,* and I've never been more excited or optimistic about what we have to build. This is why I have decided to ask our COO, Dick Costolo, to become Twitter's CEO. Starting today, I'll be completely focused on product strategy.[2]

Takeaways

1. A dead battery cannot jump-start another. If you're not fully engaged yourself, you won't be able to implement the ideas in this book.
2. Take your engagement pulse regularly and act appropriately to realign and refuel.
3. Don't go it alone. Ask for feedback or help in determining the actions you can take to increase your engagement.

6

Culture

A strong culture has a unique absorptive power to congregate people. Employees no longer need to be compelled to work hard but do so willingly. They identify themselves with their organization, just as they do with their families and communities.[1]
—*Dr. William Mobley, professor of management at CEIBS (China Europe International Business School)*

As we discussed in Chapter 4, engagement should be a daily priority owned by every member of your workforce. Assuming you are fully engaged yourself, we can now look at one key accountability factor for senior leaders that has an impact on everyone across the enterprise: *building a culture purposefully focused on engagement.*

Beyond Petri Dishes

At its most basic, culture is the sum of an organization's practices and behaviors. It reveals itself in every decision, from what time you show up to work to whether or not you proceed with an acquisition. It can simply boil down to "This is how we do things around here."

Your organization has a culture whether you like it or not; there is no such thing as a culture-less organization. Company founders and CEOs take the lead by establishing the core values, communications, and behaviors—often implicitly. But without a strong leadership hand on the helm, culture will morph organically or shift through mergers and acquisitions (there is more on this challenge at the end of the chapter).

If you let your culture evolve without supervision, you open yourself up to one that runs counter to employee engagement and business performance. But when you get culture right, it creates a foundation for high engagement that provides a competitive edge and can sustain your workforce through good times and bad.

That's because your culture, like the air you breathe, touches all employees. Culture is not an engagement program portioned out to a select group of managers, or a workplace perk that drives high employee survey scores but can succumb to budget cuts.

The Corporate Leadership Council labels culture a *public good* engagement lever. Unlike *private good* levers (e.g., coaching or career development programs), culture does not require direct investment in individual employees; it is "scalable" (by touching all levels of employees), and it requires minimal resources to maintain (providing benefits indefinitely). So if you're serious about employee engagement, it's worth taking the time to shape your culture because your efforts can provide wide-reaching, long-lasting value.

It can take years, however, to transform a weak culture into a high-performing powerhouse. Organizations that have successfully developed cultures of engagement have done so over a prolonged period of time, starting with a vision of what an engaged workplace would look like, then developing the leadership capability to build engagement in every team, department, and operating unit.

Steve Miranda is managing director of the Center for Advanced Human Resources Studies (CAHRS) at Cornell University in Ithaca, New York, and a former director at the Society of Human Resources Management (SHRM). He has seen the challenges of culture change firsthand. "Changing culture is incredibly hard, it's difficult to break old habits," Miranda says. "There's a lot of energy required. It's not simply telling people what do. . . . Leadership needs to be attentive to the effort or it will fail," he continues. "They need to listen to people doing the work. A lot of times leaders believe their people are not as smart as leadership. When it comes to their own culture, employees are always smarter."

As an aside, we acknowledge that an organization's culture is hardly homogeneous. It is made up of subcultures in regions, departments, and teams. But for the purpose of building a culture of engagement, you need to develop a unified focus and drive it across the enterprise. It may start in specific areas, but the end goal is to reach one shared definition and approach to creating a high-engagement workplace.

Eight Ways Culture Can Positively Impact Employee Engagement[2]

1. Provides meaning and emotional connection to a workforce searching for employment that offers more than just a paycheck. That connection translates into increased commitment and pride, which in turn results in higher retention and discretionary effort.

(Continued)

2. Prevents bad business practices and behavior that may not land your leaders in jail but can certainly alienate customers or employees. A strong culture weeds out leaders who do not live the core values before those leaders' behaviors damage the business and drive top talent out the door.

3. Guides and inspires employee decisions in a flatter, fast-paced workplace so that employees do all the right things when you need them to (achieving maximum contribution)—whether their manager is watching or not.

4. Encourages innovation, risk taking, and trust—all qualities characteristic of an environment that encourages employees to use their talents and discretionary effort.

5. Supports fit. Your culture helps ensure that those who do not fit leave or are not hired in the first place. When an organization focuses on engagement, not just results, hiring and firing decisions are easier to make. Better yet, bad hires often self-select out.

6. Attracts and retains star performers who not only have the skills required to achieve ambitious business goals but who are also so invigorated by the company's core beliefs that they give 110 percent.

7. Provides fixed points of reference and stability during periods of great change or crisis. Think of a lighthouse with its beacon during fog and rough seas. In the same way, a high-performance culture can keep employees motivated and aligned when business strategies are constantly shifting or marketplace pressures mount.

8. Aligns employees with diverse interests around shared goals. A carefully groomed culture creates a sense of community and teamwork, creating a common bond among individuals with different experiences and expertise. The result: a feeling of belonging to something bigger than one's self.

Six Steps

You cannot benchmark your way to a culture of engagement or try to replicate specific elements of your competitors' culture. Your culture is shaped by *your organization's* mission, values, and goals; *your organization's* definition of engagement; behaviors of *your* leaders; and the willingness and ability of *your* entire workforce to support the culture.

There are six steps you can take in the process of building your own culture of engagement. Figure 6.1 illustrates those six steps, which do not have to be done in lock-step order. Successful change does come, however, from attending to all six. And to *sustain* your culture, you will need to keep returning to the steps. You never actually complete culture change.

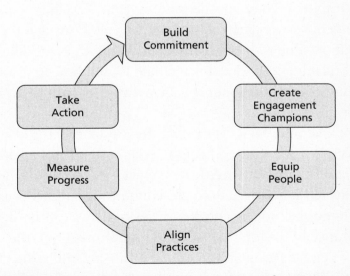

FIGURE 6.1   Six steps to building a culture of engagement.

Step 1: Build Commitment

In building commitment you need to clarify *what* you and your company are committing to—and *why* it is important.

What: A Common Definition

"Employee engagement is when an employee is motivated to create an exceptional patient experience and has an increased desire to consider our company as their career destination."
— *President, U.S.-based health care firm*

Does your organization have a shared definition and a common language for discussing engagement? Most don't. At a 2012 conference of U.S.-based HR professionals, 69 percent said that their organization did not have a clearly articulated framework for employee engagement.[3] No wonder impassioned leaderspeak about employee engagement causes eyes to glaze over or cynical workers to shrug and say, "Right. Whatever. Let me turn my attention to something tangible—like profits."

Without a common definition, your carefully compiled engagement survey data will devolve into disconnected pieces of information, absent of larger meaning. Without a carefully articulated explanation of what engagement is (and is not), any and all of the misconceptions about engagement as just happy employees will prevail.

For example, N. Balachandar, the group director of human resources at Café Coffee Day (a large coffee shop chain with headquarters in Bangalore, India), makes an important distinction between job satisfaction and commitment in his organization's framework for engagement: "Satisfaction can be fleeting, it's a transient factor," he says. "Commitment on the other hand is dependent on a set of dimensions built around clarity. Basically the role variables such as clarity and conflict drive satisfaction, which in turn impacts commitment." Balachandar adds, "Commitment is defined as quid pro quo: if the organization invests in the individual—the individual will invest in the organization."

As mentioned in Chapter 1, we have seen many definitions of engagement being used—both in the academic realm and inside organizations. The key is to have a definition that works for you in light of what your organization is trying to achieve and how engagement connects to your business strategy.

Your definition needs to meet the following criteria:

• Be actionable.

• Resonate with each and every department in every country and culture that you operate in.

• Speak of the contribution (performance) as well as the satisfaction elements of engagement—closely connecting the two.

Developing Your Engagement Lexicon

Building commitment is not a one-time task. If you are serious about sustaining a culture of engagement, the language you use can help embed engagement as a daily priority as the work gets done. Whatever definition or terms you choose, you want to create your own internal lexicon. Here are some examples that we have seen adopted:

Advocacy—the act of championing the interests of another group.

Dead battery—a manager who is not engaging her team because she is not engaged.

Managing your X—taking ownership of the factors that impact your personal engagement, then taking action to improve them.

(Continued)

Hamstering or *Crashing & Burning*—referring to behaviors associated with the less engaged levels found on the X model of engagement.

People leader—a leader who focuses on achieving high performance by helping others reach high engagement.

Pit stops—regular short engagement conversations in which employees provide feedback to their manager on their engagement drivers.

Stuck in a rut—the acknowledgment that an organization is struggling to get beyond the survey-action-plan-resurvey loop.

Victims, hostages, and *prisoners*—a key to driving engagement is making sure each individual takes accountability for his own role. We have encountered several companies that vilify victim behavior—the belief that many of the variables of engagement are out of one's control and imposed by the leadership or the broader bureaucracy.

Why: The Business Case   If you want to create a culture of engagement, you need to build the business case for doing so: Why should your leaders and workforce commit to your vision? And although there is a growing body of research that links high employee engagement and organizational performance, don't build your case around third-party data. Skeptical leaders (some of whom may be looking for an excuse to continue doing what they're doing) are likely to poke holes in the studies, most of which describe correlations and have failed to demonstrate that engagement is a leading indicator or *cause* of high performance. Instead, focus on *your organization's current strategy and metrics for success.*

How can you make the link between your organization's goals and the benefits of an aligned, thriving workforce? The following questions are critical:

1. Do you know your organization's *financial metrics*?

   (e.g., earnings per share, revenue growth, day sales outstanding)

2. Do you know your organization's *customer metrics*?

   (e.g., account acquisition, retention, penetration)

3. Do you know your organization's *value chain and productivity metrics*?

   (e.g., on-time delivery, quality indices, safety incidents, profit per employee, revenue per revenue producing position)

4. Do you know your organization's *human capital metrics*?

   (e.g., turnover, internal promotions, engagement indices)

If you are stumped by any of these questions, now is the time to find out who can help you better understand the metrics and confirm the right answer for your organization. Assuming you have clarity on the preceding four questions, there are two more:

5. Can you articulate the link between your engagement metrics and the other organizational metrics?

6. Can you speak to the challenges of engagement metrics?

Chapter 10 is devoted to these challenges if questions 5 and 6 trip you up.

Securing Senior Leader Buy-In   When you believe senior leaders understand the *what* (a common definition of engagement) and the *why* (to what end are we building a more engaged workforce?), you need to answer two more questions:

1. Who is committed?

2. What does *commitment* actually look like?

You need to be realistic about getting 100 percent support from the senior team—even if you are part of it. Some executives may be skeptical but compliant, taking a wait-and-see approach. They may not invest themselves in the effort, but will tell their people that the initiative is important and that they should all take part. You can proceed with that type of partial commitment as long as you have enough senior people in your corner and as long as the skeptics are not blocking your critical path. Some healthy cynicism can actually keep you honest.

If you don't think you have commitment yet—either hearing explicit resistance or just sensing that people are reluctantly going along with your plan—consider how you typically get buy-in from your colleagues: Do you discuss the idea with some of the leaders of disproportionate influence one-on-one? Send information (such as this book!) in advance of the next meeting? Invite a high-level engagement expert to help make the case?

Whatever you decide, it is often useful to build a network diagram of team members, their current positions, and their motivators or interests. (Most project management methodologies provide good frameworks for influence network mapping and stakeholder analysis.) When it comes to getting people excited about the topic, we recommend you reframe the conversation (see the sidebar that follows).

If you can't get commitment, you need to be realistic about why—and what you can do. Sometimes the issue is not about buy-in or even the topic of engagement but a deeper problem of senior team dysfunction.

We observed a stalled initiative at a major bank where the CEO and the chairman of the board were keen to build engagement to improve performance at the branch level. One of their star players was the executive in charge of all retail branches. He was one of the biggest cynics when it came to the importance of engagement. A firm believer in Theory X,[4] the executive was simply a roadblock. No progress will be made until he is either replaced or somehow persuaded of the value of investing in engagement.

Best Practice: Reframe the Conversation

Sometimes the best way to build your case for engagement is to take metrics, which may be disputed, out of the equation. Instead, appeal to the hearts and minds of your fellow leaders and workforce with the following process of inquiry:

- Have you ever been engaged?
- Have you ever seen anyone else who is engaged?
- Have you seen the impact that you or others have achieved when engaged?
  - Why would you not want more of those experiences happening in our organization?
  - Picture an environment where individuals are highly satisfied in their work, aligned with organizational priorities, and making a maximum contribution to our success. Who would not want that?

To date, no hard-nosed business leader has ever told us, "Not me."

Step 2: Create Engagement Champions

Unless your organization is small, you cannot build a culture of engagement on your own, even with the support of senior leaders. You need engagement champions. Champions (some firms call them ambassadors) can help:

- Bring the company's message to the rest of your organization
- Educate colleagues on what engagement is, why it is important, and how to influence it
- Help leaders interpret, communicate, and act on survey findings
- Support managers as they discuss engagement and create action plans with their teams
- Keep executives and managers accountable for playing the roles you required to make engagement a daily priority
- Support your HR team (which often takes the lead in engagement initiatives) in gathering insights and feedback from the front lines

Engagement champions should possess these 11 qualities:

1. A belief in the business benefits of employee engagement
2. A high level of personal engagement
3. An understanding of the challenges that line managers face in simultaneously delivering results and developing more passionate, engaged team members
4. Knowledge of your organization's employee engagement survey process and most recent findings
5. Experience with all levels in the workforce, including senior executives
6. Credibility across different functions or business units
7. Strong presentation and influencing skills
8. Comfort with your organization's scorecard or metrics
9. Passion for helping others progress and grow
10. The ability to facilitate, coach, and consult
11. Time to devote to the endeavor

Your overall objectives and culture will determine whom you select and what they actually do. And you'll need to provide tools and training for them to fulfill this essential advocacy role. They are expected to talk the talk, walk the walk, and be vocal and visible in supporting activities that promote engagement.

For example, Maimonides Medical Center in Brooklyn, New York, in line with a larger strategy you will read about in Chapter 7, chose a cross-section of union and management employees to play the role of engagement ambassadors. This group has been crucial in helping the organization introduce the concept of employee engagement. They have also helped to overcome the many challenges to survey completion that exist in a hospital environment: unfamiliarity with survey tools used in more corporate settings, language barriers (Maimonides' workforce speaks 26 different languages), a pressure-filled 24/7 environment, and large numbers of employees who don't use computers during their work and who, therefore, need to use a computer lab to complete the survey.

"We have such a diverse workforce and variety of positions," says Pam Brier, the president and CEO. "To build commitment and create a common language of engagement throughout the medical center, we needed to ensure the engagement ambassadors represented key employee segments. They know the issues. They speak the language and have the trust of their peers."

An American IT services firm in the financial services industry has been using champions to boost engagement as well. Sixteen business unit leaders were selected and trained to play the role to ensure a consistent approach with local nuances. The internal OD consultant in charge of the initiative explains, "We wanted them to be the go-to people and be close to the culture."

The OD consultant says the process overall has been successful, and when she hears of a struggling manager or concern about engagement, she calls in the appropriate champion (called, as Maimonides does, an ambassador) to handle the situation. (One situation featured a manager scolding his team with a well-intentioned but off-strategy message: "We're doing this engagement thing. If you don't like it, I need to show you the door.")

"You need to choose your champions and ambassadors wisely," the consultant continues. "We have found that one or two people aren't really cut out for it or don't have the time or reputation to be as effective as we need them to be. In the future, my team will work more closely with our business partners to identify champions."

Local Impact of Impassioned Communication

The following ambassador message was published in an internal department newsletter at the IT services firm we described. This was not a corporate-sponsored communication, but an example of local advocacy for higher employee engagement.

Let me start by saying I'm a realist about engagement. It is a very difficult task to improve levels of contribution and satisfaction for over 2,000 associates. That being said, I honestly don't think we have a choice. We can't maintain status quo and expect to retain the best associates or be competitive in the marketplace. There are just too many companies eager to have our customers and staff. We must act.

So just exactly how are we going to accomplish this? Well, we expect the majority of associates will have been to a local team meeting by the end of April. I can guess what some of you are thinking. Team meetings, that's their answer? This is obviously not the case.

The secret sauce about this engagement process is we ALL share in the communication and commitments. There will be meetings to discover our barriers and potential solutions, but that's not where it ends. Commitments will be made and follow-up is mandatory for everyone. Following the team meetings, there will be individual conversations designed to provide even more clarity on associate obstacles and opportunities. You might be asked questions like "What do you need your manager to do more of? How about less of?" or "What skills and knowledge would you like to use more?" Each of us will go through this process, regardless of role or tenure. Engagement must occur on all levels to be successful.

Quite a time investment, isn't it? You are guaranteed to attend at least two meetings and there is reasonable chance you might attend more. If we do this across the organization, is it even conceivable to not see improvement by year end? Unfortunately, the answer is yes and my reason for saying so might surprise you. It's simple—poor communication.

We all demand good communication and complain when it doesn't occur in a timely fashion. Interestingly, we often fail to see how we contribute to communication failures. In the context of engagement, poor communication might prevent the most vexing concerns from being raised in a meeting. We might think our issue "goes without saying" or that someone else will raise it. Only a portion of the issues raised during this process can be solved, but none of the unspoken concerns will be addressed. Help make this process successful by contributing.

Engagement Champions versus High-Potential Employees   It may be tempting to think that high-potential employees would make good engagement champions. After all, they are keen to gain exposure across the organization and are usually higher profile then their peers. Furthermore, they are motivated to make a difference, to develop personally, and to learn and apply new ideas. In practice, however, we have found that employees identified as high potentials are sometimes viewed with cynicism by others as the wannabe CEOs. As a result, they can make poor ambassadors for your engagement effort.

This is not to say that high-potential employees don't have a role to play. They represent a strategic population, which we'll explore later in this chapter. Weave engagement content into other development efforts for them. If you're rolling out engagement education for the workforce at large, consider training them first. They are your high performers and you need them fully engaged. And while they may not officially be the go-to people for engagement, they do display many of the qualities of engagement champions. If equipped properly, they can informally help to infuse engagement into your culture.

Employee Champions in China: The Spiritual Leaders

Red Star Macalline, China's largest furniture retailer, taps into a common cultural paradigm to support and guard its unique and purposeful culture. This is a paradigm that may be hard to grasp for a Western audience, but whose significance is not lost on Red Star's workforce.

In traditional Chinese military structures, each unit has two leaders: a military strategist and a spiritual leader.

If there is dissent in the ranks, the soldiers can turn to the spiritual leader for counsel.

"The thinking at the top needs execution at the front line," says Ann Huang, senior HR director. "Having two leaders in each department guarantees an execution on strategy but also retention of our company culture. If people understand the essence as well as the strategy, then they will buy in."

Red Star is not the only Chinese firm to deploy this duality of leadership roles. Even start-up Chinese firms, such as global e-commerce portal Alibaba.com, use a similar structure. "Alibaba's CEO was fired for not guarding their company's values. It is a company we watch closely and take inspiration from, so that was a big lesson for us," says Huang.

"Another example comes from the Chinese milk producers who let their guard down and allowed tainted milk into their distribution system," Huang continues. "From examples like these, we understand how quickly issues can arise if we don't have a value set to guide our behaviors, and how quickly 26 years of effort can be destroyed."

Step 3: Equip People

Chapter 4 describes the roles and responsibilities that individuals, managers, and executives need to play in keeping engagement top of mind as a daily priority that is not separated from the work. It may seem obvious, but if you need people to play particular roles, you must prepare them to do so. *Everyone* needs to understand those expectations and be prepared to behave as required. Throughout this book we touch on the skills, capabilities, and preparedness required to put your organization on the path to an effective engagement culture. Here is a recap:

Executives

- Understand and articulate the definition of engagement.
- Talk about the correlation of engagement to business results in the context of the organization's current strategy and metrics.
- Create an environment of trust that fuels engagement.
- Set and communicate a clear *and compelling* direction for the organization.
- Hold managers accountable for playing *their* role.
- Embrace their personal role in fostering the engagement as managers.
- Take control of their engagement as individuals.

Managers

- Understand and articulate the definition of engagement.
- Understand the individual engagement drivers of team members.
- Coach team members to higher levels of engagement, supporting them in their efforts to achieve maximum contribution *and* satisfaction.
- Hold individuals accountable for owning their own engagement and supporting the engagement of others.
- Take control of their engagement as individuals.

Individuals

- Understand and articulate the definition of engagement.
- Take ownership of their own engagement.
- Understand their own engagement drivers *and* the organization's definition of success.
- Take action on their own and, as appropriate, with the help of their teammates and manager.

Starting at the Top   When you are building a culture of engagement it makes sense to start with the people at the top who set the tone of your workplace: your executives. They have the most comprehensive role: to create an environment that fuels engagement, coach their own direct reports, and stay engaged themselves. The checklist in the Appendix (*Do Your Executives Create a Culture that Fuels Engagement?*) can help you determine which leadership strengths you can leverage and where you should focus development activities.

Case Study: Equipping a Decentralized Group of Leaders

CRC Health Group is the leading provider in the United States of treatment and educational programs for adults and youth who are struggling with behavioral issues, chemical dependency, eating disorders, obesity, pain management, or learning disabilities.

When the organization began building a culture of engagement, they implemented a nine-month development process to ensure that leaders could meet this challenge. Because CRC Health's facilities are spread out across the United States, they used a blend of online activities, virtual learning, and in-person workshops at regularly scheduled leadership meetings to build and sustain momentum.

The executive team first came together to review engagement findings, identify immediate actions to take as a team, and commit to a common definition and goals for engagement.

(Continued)

The top 400 leaders participated in a virtual, interactive overview about their responsibilities as leaders. This webcast established common language for engagement and expectations for their involvement in the leadership development initiative. Four to six weeks later they completed a virtual learning experience to help them manage their own engagement (no dead batteries here!).

At their next national leadership meeting, the leaders attended a one-day workshop on how to coach their employees to higher levels of engagement. In the process, they received feedback on the coaching needs of their people, following the premise that if engagement is an individualized equation, coaching needs to be an individualized approach. The leaders followed up with their teams after the workshop through one-on-one engagement partnership discussions. They used "virtual cohort groups" to learn from one another's experiences. These peer check-in meetings helped drive leader accountability for their role in increasing engagement and prevented day-to-day priorities from pushing engagement off their leadership radar. (Online tracking of partnership discussions also encouraged accountability.)

A few months later, leaders participated in another in-person learning experience, which focused on broader leadership concepts like authenticity and community building, with an overarching challenge: Why should anyone be led by you?

Creating Storytellers   Culture change requires more than communications about what engagement is and why it is important. You need to be able to *translate* your words into experiences that employees can relate to and *inspire* them to change their behavior. Storytelling is an effective technique for achieving these goals, and many organizations with purposeful cultures begin formal and informal business meetings with stories of what engagement looks like—and can achieve. Storytelling is a powerful way to make strategies and organizational values come alive, and it is explored in more depth in Chapter 7.

Your executives and managers need to weave relevant engagement-in-action examples into communications. Great day at work examples (described in Chapter 2) are useful here. So are the answers that you hear when you pose the questions to reframe the conversation when you build commitment. Stories will help ensure buy-in as effectively (if not more) than compelling metrics and provide momentum to your efforts. As executive coach Pearce explains, "To most of us, stories are reality; certainly much more so than some concepts for data or a few insights."[5]

Targeting Strategic Populations   When you're trying to change culture, it's useful to identify the areas of your organization where you can obtain the most traction and quick successes. High-potential employees, as mentioned earlier, are an excellent segment of the population to train—especially with respect to taking control of their own engagement. The more they understand their personal definition of success and job fit, the better able they will be to successfully step into the roles you need them to play—and suggest alternatives to moves that would be career killers for them and poor results for you.

As you consider equipping your managers to support their team's engagement, think about training the managers who work in

- Departments that are most critical to your current strategy
- Areas with the greatest impact on customers
- Units that already manage with metrics like revenue and customer satisfaction (and offer the best chance at measuring the return on your engagement efforts)

- Locations with decent engagement levels (to build on strengths for maximum impact)
- Groups that will be experiencing significant change (and therefore need the foundation of high engagement to stay productive)
- High-visibility and credible departments or locations that can become your flagship examples of engagement in action

Step 4: Align Practices

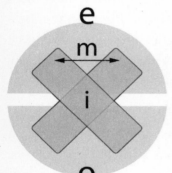

It's not enough for all levels (I, M, E) of your workforce to *own* engagement. Successful culture change requires that your operational engine drive engagement as well as your strategic priorities. Too often, engagement is undermined by policies and practices that drive only results.

The acid test may be this: If, in the course of your engagement efforts, you heard of a long-established policy or process that ran counter to your engagement initiative, what would your reaction be? Will people need to get engaged despite this policy, or is it the policy that needs to change? You may be thinking the latter, but too often poor organizational practices prevail and engagement is expected to work around it.

When that happens, savvy independent-minded managers may succeed—like Marshall B. Farrer. Farrer is managing director for Brown Forman (Australia/New Zealand) (one of the 10 largest global spirits companies, with brands that include Jack Daniels and Southern Comfort). Two-thirds of Farrer's 170 workers are in sales—most working out of their homes. He tries to buffer his team from the distractions of the larger organization and maintain the entrepreneurial spirit that fuels success: "We try not to be corporate. This is not reinforced by any policy or procedure—we just don't act that way. We never let a policy get in the way of a good decision." If a policy seems counter productive, they review as a team to gain a collective approach that works.

Rather than relying on managers like Farrer, you're better off fixing the practices that don't drive your goals.

Look at it from your organization's perspective. Which of these policies or business practices fully support engagement in your organization?

1. Internal communications
2. Employer branding
3. Compensation and benefits
4. Employee experience (recruiting, hiring, onboarding, workplace policies)
5. Performance management
6. Rewards and recognition
7. Training and development (career, skills, growth assignments)

Critically examining the practices in your organization will allow you to identify and address barriers to higher engagement. The most common culprits: career development (or lack thereof), performance management, rewards and recognition. We will touch on just a few here.

Onboarding and Staff Meetings to Define Maximum Contribution

The Ritz-Carlton is a U.S.-based hotel chain that differentiates itself through superior customer experiences. The firm is very clear what behaviors drive guest satisfaction and reflect their well-respected brand.

Sandra Sadowski, the director of spa and fitness at the Ritz-Carlton New York, Central Park, describes the hotel's culture as deliberately formal and an atmosphere in which employees are expected to conform to high standards and expectations.

The company has 12 service values that frame its culture and inform the treatment of other employees and guests. (Service value 11, for example, is "I protect the privacy and security of our guests, my fellow employees, and the company's confidential information and assets.")

"It's something that's lived every day, and it's about respect," Sadowski says. "There's a detail-oriented style and way of treating each other. Our motto is 'ladies and gentlemen serving ladies and gentlemen.' It's a much more formal environment than other hotels."

"The Ritz-Carlton sometimes has a reputation as being stuffy or old," she says. "But we think engaging with a guest while still being refined is important."

The company therefore aligns new hires with its brand from day one through formal onboarding activities. The hotel chain then maintains alignment of all 38,000 employees through regular—often daily—staff meetings.

Internal Communications: Beyond the Newsletter   The National Geographic Society in Washington, DC, is an example of an organization taking a multifaceted approach to improving its communications practices as it transforms its culture, according to Tony Sablo, the senior vice president, human resources.

One way they are improving internal communications is a complete reimagining of the company's intranet by making it more personalized. They have hired a director of internal communications who is working with a staff-led advisory council to make the platform more user-friendly. The site, now known as NG Connect, includes staff videos that celebrate employees' accomplishments, both in and outside the workplace.

Sablo says that CEO John Fahey communicates to the staff through many channels, including his own blog and informal weekly coffee meeting held with small groups of staff members (usually 30 or less to allow for dialogue, not just a one-way message). "There's much more frequent communication and the feeling that we're making a difference in a broader sense; that management cares about doing better," says Sablo.

Leave No Stone Unturned . . . Organizational practices do not have to appear broken to be falling short as reinforcers of your employee engagement goals. The most obvious problems will be called out in your employee engagement survey findings: career development, rewards and recognition, and compensation often make the list.

Aligning your practices to help achieve the goal of a high-engagement culture requires the discipline to step back and assess whether the practices and policies you take for granted are driving the behaviors you desire.

Case Study: Aligning Practices from the Start

When Etihad Airways in the United Arab Emirates was planning a new call center, its goal was to create a workplace with high levels of engagement and further its objective of hiring more Emirati employees. (In a country where the workforce is 80 percent foreign workers, competition for local Emirati talent is fierce.)

(Continued)

They realized women in second-tier cities were an untapped labor market. Because Emiratis can go to university for free, these women were well educated and often multi-lingual. Yet many did not work because employers had failed to come up with options that met their needs to balance job and family responsibilities. If the airline could bring the work to this population and craft an appropriate work environment and job scope, they believed women would join the Etihad workforce—and stay.

The large metro centers of Dubai and Abu Dhabi are fairly progressive, and most work environments include both male and female employees working alongside each other. Smaller cities in the United Arab Emirates tend to be more conservative and provide less opportunity. Women are much more comfortable working in an all-female environment, so Etihad created a high-tech purpose-built call center in Al-Ain, 160 km from headquarters.

Etihad then designed work shifts around family and school hours since the women they sought to attract still had important roles to play at home. The result: the firm was able to build, recruit, and fully staff their call center with committed, largely Emirati employees in record time. Retention is high because the work is designed to fit the needs of the employees. By not forcing employees into jobs that did not fit their social or family context, Etihad was able to ensure high levels of engagement.

CEO James Hogan said, "We appreciate the different values and approach that Emirati women consider when entering the workforce, and the design of the center aims to ensure its female-only structure and opportunities for flexible working hours allow women to develop their career, while creating a sustainable work, life, and home balance."

Step 5: Measure Progress

So how will you know if you are succeeding in creating a culture of engagement? Engagement surveys, pulse surveys, and the metrics you use already to run your business can provide insights. (Note that we did *not* say, "Benchmark your engagement levels against your competitors.")

Engagement Surveys   Many companies conduct comprehensive engagement surveys without taking any of the other steps we have described to build a culture of engagement. These organizations see surveys as the beginning and end of their initiative, devoting all their resources to measurement without taking action. That obviously is not enough. Without a foundation of commitment, shared ownership, and aligned practices, regular surveys become an irrelevant exercise.

In the context of culture building, we are not suggesting that you eliminate engagement surveys. Instead, follow the best practices provided in Chapter 11 to efficiently run them and maximize the insights they can provide.

Pulse Surveys   Pulse surveys typically are short, to the point, and subject to change based on your most recent engagement findings and action plans. They can be designed to explore

- Points of pain identified in the last engagement survey
- Areas that your executives selected to focus on through organization-wide action planning
- How successful your efforts are at creating a culture of engagement.

The last bullet is critical, and can be measured with items such as "I understand how my company defines engagement,"

"My manager has led a team meeting about engagement in the last three months," and "I actively manage my own engagement."

What about Your Survey-Weary Workforce?   A lot of ink and consulting is devoted to methods you can use to protect your survey-weary workforce. You may have considered pulsing a random 20 percent of your workforce or following up with some departments, not others.

Our advice: don't worry about it. If you want to create a culture of engagement, pulse everyone. If you have been conducting engagement surveys without context or action, sure, your employees will be weary of being asked to participate in a process that has little to no impact on their work experience or your business. As you build commitment, refine your survey methodology, improve your communication and follow-up of findings, and create broader ownership of engagement, survey-weary employees will become a bad memory.

> There is a simple but significant way to help achieve [long-term value]: Evaluate and compensate CEOs, at least partly, on their ability to create a culture of aligned, engaged employees. That would require . . . balancing financial metrics with measures that track the ability to forge internal alignment. . . . But the missing link in CEO compensation continues to be employee engagement and satisfaction— holding the CEO accountable for creating a culture that aspires to make a lasting difference.
> —*Kenneth W. Freeman, dean of the Boston University School of Management, in Harvard Business Review blog*[6]

There is an additional benefit to pulsing: you send the message to the entire workforce that engagement continues to be a priority, that the insights are important for managing the business. Engagement is not an initiative that is going away.

Your Scorecard Stay close to the financial, customer, value chain, and human capital metrics that your organization already tracks. As Chapter 10 acknowledges, you may not be able to determine unequivocally that higher engagement is driving success, but you may be able to show a correlation between your engagement efforts and improved numbers that matter.

To start, make engagement part of the conversation.

Step 6: Take Action

If you're measuring progress toward creating a culture of engagement well, you'll end up with *actionable* insights. If you're swimming in data or at a loss on whether you're better off than six months or a year ago, Chapters 10 and 11 are for you.

Team Actions While most survey cycles include a phase of action planning, this is typically done in a survey-knows-best approach: based on the findings, organization-wide recommendations are made that managers are supposed to follow, as if some magic sauce existed that can be applied to all teams based on some simple flowchart logic or statistical analysis.

Reality isn't that simple, so you are best entrusting and empowering your managers to work with their teams to increase their engagement levels. After all, people are never more accountable for plans than the ones they create.

Encouraging dialogue and planning at the team level also provide a valuable feedback loop. Here's why: imagine your post-measurement activities to be like the sonar on a submarine. You get the results and broadcast them throughout the organization—your sonar signal goes out. It hits the ranks of managers. Now what you need is for the signal to bounce back and give you a clear picture of what happens as a result. If your sonar signal says, "Do these actions," the feedback will be, "Okay, actions done," and you will have a neat scorecard of how many managers ticked the box.

Imagine instead that your sonar signal says, "Here are the findings; we need to know what *you* think—and what you are going to do about it. Talk to your teams and record your insights and the agreements you make for increasing your team's engagement." With this second approach you get more attention and understanding of the findings, more specific insights from teams, more management and individual ownership, and more accountability.

This approach benefits from a bit of technology to support it—a simple online tool can help managers plan meetings and hold themselves and their teams accountable (as well as helping you track activities, encourage accountability, and roll-up insights and feedback), but it can be done with conversations, paper, and e-mail follow-up.

The process is simple: each manager holds a team meeting upon receiving engagement findings to discuss the results and generate ideas for increasing engagement levels.

A simple agenda for the meeting is as follows:

1. Restate the organization's definition of engagement and why engagement is important.

2. Discuss reactions to the findings candidly, identifying the most important insights related to the team's engagement.

3. Identify what *the team* can do. The manager's role here is to make sure the conversation and the actions focus on the work and do not drift off onto non-actionable items.

Changes in how the team works together or interacts with other teams is within scope, but compensation, benefits, or company strategy would be beyond reach.

4. Ask what you can start, stop, or continue doing *as a manager* to support increased team engagement. Keep the list short and actionable, and remember that you don't have to agree to all ideas. You can also come to the meeting with a few ideas of your own to test out.

5. Ask for upward feedback, for example, "What message should I share with senior leaders? What do *they* need to know about your engagement?" Pick the top two or three. This is where those issues (like compensation or strategy) that the team has no control over can be addressed.

6. Summarize agreements, recognize the team's commitment and creativity, reaffirm your commitment to their engagement and success, and schedule a follow-up meeting.

The manager then records a summary of agreements and shares it with the team. The upward feedback is recorded as well and shared with HR or online, where the information can be viewed by leaders.

These meetings are tremendous value-add in your overall engagement strategy—they are about both organizational feedback *and* commitment to action at the front line. The upward feedback is more valuable and efficient than focus groups for providing insights into additional executive and organizational actions to consider. This process will also give credence to any visible actions you undertake as a senior team—you can connect back the initiatives to explicit feedback from frontline teams.

Actions on the Front Lines   The following are examples of commitment items we have seen in our work with clients. We include these here to give you an idea of the type of feedback you are likely to get from running this exercise.

Examples of Team Commitments

- We will hold each other accountable for not slipping into contagious negativity.
- We will prioritize our work and reduce menial tasks; set boundaries to sustain a manageable work/life balance; and reduce overtime by working smarter!
- Using the new project manager role, we will try to get some of the manual issues corrected so we can work more strategically instead of putting out fires all the time.
- Celebrate every project no matter how small. We tend to say, "Good job," and then just move on to the next project. So we'll go to lunch or do something else to celebrate.
- Each team member will be held accountable to become a subject matter expert (SME) in an area by reaching out to existing SMEs and training with them.
- The team has committed to carefully considering and controlling reactions when faced with situations such as conflicting direction from managers or other leaders. This team is dedicated to working together and integrating new members into the existing team.

Examples of Manager Commitments

- I commit to improving the frequency and variety of recognition.
- I will open my calendar to all team members so they know where I am and what I am doing, and so they can make judgment calls on when to interrupt me for various issues or to set ad hoc one-on-one sessions.

- I will do one-on-ones monthly instead of every other month; look into vending machines; get the bathroom door fixed; post company mission statement and goals.

- I commit to (1) provide more specific feedback on job performance; (2) get to know them as individuals with lives outside of work; (3) maintain discipline around executing action plans; (4) be a sounding board without necessarily taking any action.

- I will go talk to the team in marketing and explain why our materials need to be turned around faster.

- I will work at least two night shifts and one weekend a month. I will also remain positive when reviewing DOT regulations and company policies.

- I promise to inform upper management of the responsibilities of this team to help them understand the pressure this team goes through to meet deadlines and produce quality products.

Examples of Upward Feedback to Senior Leaders

- We believe the senior leaders should hold the company more accountable for living the value of Customer Focus.

- We want more frequent communication from senior management (people *loved* the town hall and would like to see them way more often). Senior leaders should share why/ how decisions are made (e.g., pay increases won't happen because we do not want to lay off anyone). Don't sugarcoat messages.

- We have lost eight people in the past two years due to layoffs, attrition, and reorganization, yet our responsibilities continue to grow. We are spread too thin, our skills are becoming diluted, we no longer have time to be proactive, we are being asked to do and remember too much, resulting in a higher rate of errors. We are no longer able to provide outstanding customer service.

- Employees stated, "Pizza parties are nice but we would rather receive discounts on our gasoline or gift cards," and "Why install a new flat-screen TV in the break room, when we would rather have the money and don't take breaks in there?"

- Overall, the work environment is good and the staff likes and respects each other. The subject of meaningful raises was brought up several times.

- The staff thinks that the current salary ranges are not in alignment with wages in our area. They also think that hourly employees should be included in the community bonus structure. They feel less valued because they are not included.

- Your executive briefings refer to various senior executives. We don't know who they are, even though their photos were included.

Fusing Disparate Cultures: Mergers and Acquisitions

You've spent years building a culture of engagement, celebrated for its nimbleness, intelligent employees, and inspiring leaders. Then suddenly that culture is threatened after a high-profile merger and/or acquisition. A business can suddenly have thousands of new employees used to doing things in a completely different way.

"Every company has a different culture," says J. Thomas Richardson, senior vice president and infrastructure strategy/architecture executive at Bank of America, based in Denver, Colorado. "B of A is a melting pot that has tried to preserve the integrity of an organization and its people as best as we can whether you agree with the acquisition or not."

In the last ten years Bank of America has made multiple high-profile acquisitions, including FleetBoston Financial in 2004, credit card giant MBNA in 2005, Countrywide Financial in 2008, and later that year, famously, Merrill Lynch.

Richardson noticed a difference in internal communications styles after several of Bank of America's acquisitions in the late 2000s.

At one of the new companies, employee communications were limited by hierarchy. "They needed direct permission if they wanted to reach out to their boss's boss," says Richardson. "Not doing so was a recipe for career suicide, an unwritten diplomatic protocol. Years later, we're still dealing with that to some extent, although it exists to a much lesser degree. We're working with people, getting them to communicate across boundaries."

Miranda, of CAHRS, looks back at an acquisition when he was at Lucent Technologies in 1999 that upended the company culture:

> When the company acquired Ascend Communications, a company with 2,000 employees, there was a feeling that we would need to be more like them—faster and more nimble. There was a gross underestimation of the inertia of a company with 120,000 employees moving more nimbly. It was very tough. 2,000 people can't try to change 120,000.

Takeaways

- Culture is there whether you have deliberately shaped it or not. It makes good business sense to make sure your culture is working for you—to drive high performance and engagement.

- Get your culture right and it can carry you through good times and bad.

- You need to build commitment to engagement in the beginning—and never stop.

- Choose respected, passionate, and engaged colleagues as your engagement champions.

- Equip everyone in the workforce for the roles you need them to play (I, M, E), but start with the leaders at the top.

- Align your policies and business practices to drive engagement in addition to your strategic objectives.

- Measure progress as often as possible. Don't rely solely on engagement surveys.

- As you gather insights, revise and ramp up what you're doing to build commitment, create engagement champions, equip people, and align practices. The circle in Figure 6.1 means *keep going*.

- Recognize the challenges to employee engagement presented by acquisitions and mergers.

7

Seems Kind of Obvious: Align Your Employees!

I am no different than the average employee. If I had an understanding of what the organization needed, why the organization was doing what it was doing, and how my role and actions fit in, then I was super engaged.

—*David Norton, former group chairman,*
global pharmaceuticals, Johnson & Johnson

If engagement in your organization needs a boost, there is a better solution than installing latte machines or allowing employees to bring their dogs to work: align them to what is most important to your organization.

Getting all employees aligned to your strategy, mission, and values is something you should do even if you don't give a hoot about engagement. It is a requirement for high performance.

(Of course, if you believe that your employees are lucky they all have jobs and that they don't need to worry about the big picture, you probably wouldn't be reading Chapter 7 in a book on engagement.) After all, you and your colleagues have invested a lot of time in setting the organization's course, and you need every member of the workforce rowing in sync, in the same direction, at full power, to attain your goals.

Lack of alignment is the silent killer of engagement. It is overlooked because:

- Soft definitions of engagement (which we discussed in Chapter 1) emphasize satisfaction and don't address contribution and performance.
- Leaders assume it exists already, since strategy and performance are what leaders already understand and know how to drive (so the thinking goes).

It's unfortunate that alignment is taken for granted, because maximum contribution (half of the engagement equation) can only be achieved if employees are crystal clear on the organization's definition of success, how they fit in, and what they need to do every day to drive organizational objectives.

Alignment with your organization's interests and goals can also:

- Move Honeymooners & Hamsters into full engagement by providing focus for their discretionary effort or misplaced enthusiasm.
- Ensure that the Engaged continue to perform at high levels.
- Fuel employees' emotional commitment with your organization by providing meaning and a sense of what it can do for people (the greater good).

- Feed the symbiotic relationship of satisfaction and contribution, since employees who are not confident that their hard work actually matters will eventually become less satisfied.

Foundations for Alignment

Before we get into detail on what you need to do, let's look at the factors that shape your organization's definition of success:

- *Your mission.* A mission, or purpose as some firms call it, answers the question of why your company exists. Making money doesn't qualify as the answer, although profitability is essential to your firm's survival. Your mission explains your reason for being. It doesn't have to be lofty; its mere existence serves as your organization's North Star, providing a fixed point to which your workforce can connect. Ideally, it should inform business decisions, generate customer loyalty, ignite employee passion, and inspire discretionary effort.
- *Your organizational values.* Values guide employee behavior and influence business practices as your organization delivers on its promises to customers, employees, and other stakeholders. They answer the questions: "What are your guiding principles? What are your organization's rules of the road?" While your business strategies shift to meet market demands, your core values usually don't.
- *Your goals and strategy.* Goals describe specific milestones the organization aims for in fulfilling its mission. Ideally, those goals should be shaped by a compelling long-term vision similar to the *BHAG* concept Jim Collins and Jerry Porras presented in *Built to Last* (big, hairy, audacious goal). Your strategy describes how you plan to achieve organizational

goals. Your strategy answers the questions: "Where should we focus?" and "What needs to be accomplished?"

Why the Cats Won't Herd

Getting people to work toward a singular goal is no simple task. Despite the increase in fancy performance management systems, cascading goal setting, sophisticated internal communications, and social media tools, aligning employee and organizational priorities remains difficult.

As we examine some of the most common reasons for disconnected or misaligned employees below, you should consider whether or not each is limiting your ability to create a more engaged workforce. We'll explore best practices for avoiding these pitfalls later in the chapter.

Disagreement at the Top

If senior executives are not completely aligned—whether in overt disagreement, well-intentioned confusion, or passive/aggressive compliance—employees are going to get mixed signals, at best, about what matters most to your organization. Change initiatives will stall. Worst-case scenarios include bad leader behavior and lack of collaboration across departments, both of which drive *dis*engagement and turnover.

Your Acid Test: Watch for symptoms like decisions that are revisited each time you meet, unspoken challenges or skepticism behind stated questions, overt disagreement (in comments and nonverbal behavior), silence, and lack of progress on agreed-to action items. To uncover misunderstandings, ask leaders to reiterate in their own words the intent of the strategy, the meaning of the mission, and implications for the groups of employees that they manage.

Communication Mistakes

Engaged employees understand organizational priorities, but they also *care enough* to take the right action. To create more engaged employees, leaders need to capture hearts as well as minds. Unfortunately, leadership communications often fail to achieve that type of commitment, suffering from what we call "too seldom, too much, and too dry."

- *Too seldom.* Senior teams are big on strategy, but don't adequately or frequently share it throughout the organization. One CEO said, "What do you mean people don't know the strategy? I told all the employees what the strategy was in an e-mail last year."

- *Too much.* We are certain that at least once in your career (only once if you're lucky) you have attended a 30-minute town hall meeting where a top executive speaks for 28 minutes, flashes through 80 numbers-filled slides that you can't read from the back of the room, leaving 2 minutes to answer only one question. With improvements in technology, a leader can confuse thousands of employees around the world through synchronous and asynchronous virtual presentations while uninterested employees clean out their e-mail or play games on their smartphones. This is a combination of too much and too little—too much information jammed into too little time.

- *Too dry.* Some executives actually believe that the rallying cry of increasing shareholder value is a shot of adrenalin for employees. Using the most-sophisticated business school jargon, they position strategic decisions as rational, well-researched, and a good use of the organization's best assets. The absence of inspiration ends any hope for increased engagement.

Your Acid Test: Just as recording everything you eat when you're dieting provides a reality check on the amount of food you never realized you consume each day, tracking your leadership messages can reveal how few communications are actually distributed. To gauge whether a message has been heard and understood, consider formal feedback loops (like a short online survey) or talk to employees. Ask whether they have questions, or about their level of commitment, and even about what specific details they remember from the message.

Disconnects on the Front Lines

When employees say they don't know the organization's strategy, they often mean they don't see how *their job* fits into the strategy. Norton, formerly of Johnson & Johnson, says:

> You want people who are working with you to be engaged in the central mission and how their piece of the puzzle fits. Sometimes people low down in the organization don't understand how and what they are doing fits into the bigger picture. Then they are not motivated or passionate. They may bitch and moan. They won't go the extra mile when the organization needs them to.

Even when they do understand how their job supports the organization's big picture, employees are often misguided on which of the 10 projects on their to-do list matter most. When an employee and manager are asked to identify the employee's top three priorities, there is usually agreement on only one of the three.[1]

Your Acid Test: Talk to front line managers and individual contributors. Find out whether they have received the message, understood the intent, and see how organizational imperatives shape their role. Spend more time listening than talking.

You might also pull data from your performance management system to review priorities. You will probably find irrelevant goals (most systems suffer from "garbage in, garbage out") or priorities that no longer apply in your fast-moving business environment.

George Weston Food: A Case Study

A well-planned communication strategy that has the support of the entire organization's leadership is critical to implement change. Andrew Reeves, the CEO of GWF, realized he needed to communicate a message of significance, soon after joining the company in 2011. GWF is one of Australia and New Zealand's largest food manufacturers. It employs about 6,500 people in 60 sites including sites in China and Japan.

"While our people had strong loyalty and felt part of the Weston's family business, as a manufacturer, the business had lost its way," Reeves says. "We were internally focused and too siloed; everyone had their own process and way of doing things. This meant there were lots of duplication across core processes. We didn't have a strong focus on our customers or the external market."

Best Practices

Books dedicated exclusively to strategy alignment, values-based cultures, and leadership communication are widely available, so our ambition is not to cover these topics in too much depth here. But we do want to give you some insights into how leadership behaviors and communications can help improve alignment and therefore engagement.

Align Senior Leaders

The best way to ensure that your executives are aligned with your strategy, values, and mission is to involve these leaders in their creation. If your mission and values have been in place for a while, use them. They should serve as a touchstone for executive decisions and communications.

- How does your current strategy link to the organization's mission?
- How do important decisions align with your organization's espoused values? (If you can't make the connection, the decision may have negative consequences.)
- How has each leader communicated the big picture relationship of mission, values, and strategy to their employees?

Don't take alignment with strategy for granted. One CEO we interviewed found alarming disconnects during one-on-one meetings with each of his team members about short-term priorities. He thought he had been clear in setting the direction for the organization a few months earlier, but some executives had translated his vision into departmental priorities that he disagreed with.

So if you have shifted strategies to respond to market conditions, check in with your top leaders.

- How do they feel about the new direction?
- How have those changes been communicated?
- How are departments and business units altering their priorities?

If a decision was hotly debated, deal quickly with dissent, and don't allow meetings to end without every person's articulated commitment to the plan of action. This approach will enable senior-level colleagues to hold one another accountable for agreements made.

Pam Brier, the president and CEO of Maimonides Medical Center in Brooklyn, New York, dealt with high-level resistance to a new strategy successfully. When Brier came to the hospital in 1995, she found what one employee described as a "culture of nastiness" that was undermining quality of care and patient satisfaction. She decided to develop a labor–management strategic alliance based on the premise "good things will happen when non-management employees have the opportunity to improve things." But Brier did not have the immediate support of her team. She describes the pushback:

> When we started, a senior manager said to me, "What are you doing—you are going to get the union involved in decisions?" There are degrees of participation, and I think that some of the best ideas come from the people who do the work: the housemaid, environmental worker on the unit, the nurse or nurse's aide. They have plenty to say. If there is mutuality of respect, then you can reach decisions.

Brier's strategy of involving union members in the decision-making process receives accolades today and has allowed tremendous positive change to take place. But getting the whole senior team on board took time, required debate, and in some cases, new executives who shared Brier's vision of success based on a collaborative relationship with the unions.

Communicate Deliberately and Often

Every organization has its barriers to effective communications. You know yours. Create an approach that addresses them.

How does an airline, for instance, ensure that teams of people (part office staff, part ground workers, part 30,000-feet-in-the-air flight crew) scattered across remote locations remain connected with organizational imperatives?

"In an airline, you can't conduct one town hall meeting," explains K.S. Bakshi, vice president of HR at IndiGo, a private, low-cost airline based in India. "It's a 24/7 operation and distributed across regions, even countries. So our executive team has to go to where the people are. We inculcated a practice of reaching out as often as we can, and set the target for the senior team of visiting all 27 stations twice a year."

When you need to communicate a new decision or strategic direction, make sure your plan leverages all the tools your organization has: e-mail, videoconferences, social media, and in-person meetings. Match the right communication vehicle with the right executive.[2] Include feedback loops and checkpoints to make sure that the message is being heard, understood, and acted upon.

Finally, don't abdicate sole responsibility to your communications department. Beyond these deliberate communication activities, leaders need to provide ad-hoc reinforcement in every conversation. Conversations help ensure a two-way flow of information, which is critical for building commitment and translating organizational mandates into daily priorities. When leaders think they're done, they still need to keep going. So let's take a closer look at the content of effective leadership communications.

Communicate for Clarity and Inspiration

In addition to the *what* of a decision, leaders need to include the *why*. The why adds commitment to clarity. And to be really effective, the why must go beyond the organization's goals to include why leaders personally care and what the organization (or the market or the world) will look like when success is achieved.

Show the Math　As a leader you know why you've made a particular decision. You and your colleagues may have spent weeks or months analyzing the issue and debating the new direction. By the time you're ready to announce it, you want to jump to action. Why waste time talking?

Your workforce, however, needs to catch up if they are to take appropriate action. They need to digest the *why* behind the *what* if they are to commit. And if you don't make that connection explicit, we guarantee they will assume a less-than-honorable hidden agenda or draw conclusions you would never dream of.

So you need to *show the math* for your decisions. Think back to middle school when your math teacher required you to not only provide the answer to a problem—but also the process by which you arrived at your answer. This requirement enabled teachers to determine whether you were applying concepts correctly (even if you ended up with the wrong solution). In the workplace, that concept plays out as taking the time to explain the process and rationale for decisions and overtly illustrating how the organization's strategy, mission, and values are supported.

Tell a Story　If engagement seems like a soft topic to hard-nosed executives, then the topic of storytelling will seem positively esoteric. Yet every organization is a tribe, and every tribe has its stories. Storytelling helps bring intangible concepts alive ("here's what our values in action look like") to drive alignment. K. Ramkumar, executive director for human resources at India's largest private bank, ICICI Bank, explains,

> I have not seen a more powerful way of preserving the culture. Our company is a compendium of stories and people are adding new stories every day—you could almost say that we are cultish. Some stories you will hear repeated include the time we made a transaction miscalculation which cost the bank $7 million. When our CEO found out

he instructed that we need to investigate the issue but avoid making anybody a scapegoat. That was a strong story to explain the culture we aspire to.

Executive coach and leadership guru Terry Pearce says in his book *Leading Out Loud*, that storytelling is all about creating the limbic resonance that helps others *feel* your message.

The mind looks for proof, the heart looks for passion. The mind weighs facts, the heart acts on faith. The mind looks for purpose, the heart seeks meaning. The mind believes, the heart trusts.

According to Pearce, stories must be

- Relevant
- First person (or have a personal connection)
- Sensory rich (because detail brings stories to life)
- Related from memory
- Filled with facts and feelings[3]

Be Authentic   Pearce and other experts provide detailed insights into the importance of authenticity in leadership. Our goal in this chapter, then, is to remind you that when you explain what an organizational initiative means to you personally (or why you personally believe it is exciting and likely to succeed) you increase your chances of inspiring employees to contribute their discretionary effort toward organizational goals. (Check out the Appendix for ideas on how to bring your personal commitment as a leader into your message.)

Beyond Leadership Behavior

Encourage Manager-Employee Dialogue   Two-way conversations between a manager and his or her direct reports remain the most effective way to translate organizational imperatives to individual jobs and daily priorities. Without such regular dialogue, you will continue to find employees at all levels in your organization working on the wrong things or so disconnected that they are disengaged. We explore these crucial conversations in Chapter 8.

Fix Your Performance Management System Most corporate performance management systems don't work! Buck Blessing, founder of BlessingWhite, said more than two decades ago, "If one were making a list of the great failures in human history, performance appraisals would have to be right there with the *Titanic*, new math, and Napoleon's Moscow campaign."

Managers hate annual performance appraisals. Employees dread them. The systems in place amount to administrative nightmares that have little to do with performance, much less engagement. In theory, your system should help ensure that employees' goals support the organization's imperatives.

Your system's blend of human/high-tech elements, measurement tools, ratings, and training needs to fit your culture. By all means, check out what works in other organizations. Just remember that performance management systems need to be custom-tailored.

Ultimately, the effectiveness of this (potentially powerful) alignment tool depends on the conversations that take place between employees and managers, not the rate of compliance. Your system needs to be less about online forms and awkward annual reviews. Instead, focus on continuous dialogue and partnership about what matters most to the employee and the organization. Chapter 8 contains insights into the types of manager-employee conversations that need to occur on an ongoing basis because alignment needs to happen more than once a year.

Clarify Your Mission and Values   If you don't have a published mission and core values, identify and define them to help employees connect emotionally to your organization (and hence, boost engagement). Although the process can be time consuming, you won't actually start with a blank slate. Your organization has rules of the road even if they are unspoken. Rather than provide detail on this approach, we encourage you to check out one of the resources mentioned in the endnotes.[4]

Examples of Missions and Values

Consider the following examples from two successful but very different organizations.

The mission statements published on the firms' websites reflect two clear corporate identities and answer the question, "What is your reason for being?"

- American financial services firm Charles Schwab & Co.'s mission is, according to its website, "To help everyone be financially fit." This short statement is further explained with a quote from the firm's founder and chairman, Charles R. Schwab: "All of us at Schwab come to work every day focused on our purpose: to help everyone be financially fit. That may seem like a simple statement, but it has a very powerful impact on how we do business, and on our potential for continued profitable growth."

- France-based LVMH Group (known for global luxury brands like Louis Vuitton, Moët, and TAG Heuer) lists the following mission: "To represent the most refined qualities of Western 'Art de Vivre' around the world. LVMH must continue to be synonymous with both elegance and creativity. Our products, and the cultural values they embody, blend tradition and innovation, and kindle dream and fantasy."

Likewise, the organizational values below reflect the cultures of their respective organizations, as guiding principles for how employees should live out their employer's mission.

Charles Schwab & Co.

- Provide clients with the most ethical financial services.
- Be fair, empathetic, and responsive in serving our clients.
- Strive relentlessly to improve what we do and how we do it.
- Respect and reinforce our fellow employees and the power of teamwork.
- Always earn and be worthy of our clients' trust.

LVMH Group

- Be creative and innovate.
- Aim for product excellence.
- Bolster the image of our brands with passionate determination.
- Act as entrepreneurs.
- Strive to be the best in all we do.

Case Study: Mission Is Not Enough

One organization that successfully wrestled with workforce alignment is the Starlight Foundation of Australia, which runs programs in pediatric hospitals. Starlight's *captains* are professional actors, comedians, and musicians, who work in-residence in hospitals, touring the children's wards, or working out of dedicated Starlight Rooms where sick kids go to have fun and just be kids.

Engagement of individuals in a charity has its own dynamic: people join charities because they believe in the mission of the organization but that does not mean they are committed to the process or the ways of working. Consequently, people tend to pursue their own agenda if they feel it furthers what they understand as the mission of the organization. "This is understandable," says CEO Louise Baxter. "But we are still an organization, not a collection of free agents. Like any organization we have a need for consistency and process to stay efficient. This is no different from any for-profit corporation, but we have no real buffer, so we have to act early to keep everybody on track."

In 2009 the organization had slumped into a poorly led, low engagement mess. Turnover was high, employee engagement was low, and lackluster performance was the accepted norm. Charitable donations dried up.

"The organization had lost its direction," Baxter points out. So from 2010 to 2012, Baxter and her new leadership team drove a return to its core practices.

An initiative called the Starlight Experience was begun, focusing on 100 percent advocacy for three key stakeholder groups: the children, donors/supporters, and the Starlight team and employees.

All employees were asked to take a pledge connected to the purpose of the organization. The management team in turn committed themselves to changing the way the organization was led. "We needed to know that everybody on the payroll was committed to positive advocacy," Baxter says. "We knew it would take time and nobody expected 100 percent advocacy from day one."

Starting with the senior leadership team, Baxter drove home the message that cracks at the executive team level can become chasms within the rank and file. There was an urgent need for consistent messaging and openness.

The turnaround took three years. In 2010, the organization experienced a 43 percent turnover, but by 2012, it had cut that turnover number in half. Donations skyrocketed with double-digit growth. Morale improved, individual employee engagement increased, and advocacy for the three key stakeholders had become the core driver of success for Starlight.

Baxter says, "I can gauge engagement based on the number of letters coming in thanking us for the work that we do. Not just in terms of the number of letters but the specifics in the messages. People will reference specific individuals and thank us for the care and attention that one person specifically displayed."

Case Study: Alignment at the Local Level

Solving the engagement equation is contingent on empowering leaders to make your organization's business strategy work at a local level. Sometimes it also requires that leaders take initiative to inspire and focus employees around common goals while the larger organizational strategy is being sorted out thousands of miles away. This story illustrates how insights from this chapter can be successfully applied on a smaller scale.

Daryl Sisson is an example of a leader who did just that. He leads a go-to-market channel known as Direct for Thomson Reuters Asia Pacific. Direct is Thomson Reuters' virtual go-to-market capability, remotely managing thousands of customer accounts and millions of dollars in revenue. The group is also responsible for new client acquisition and lead generation. Clients are spread across Asia, so there are three regional hubs in Sydney, Tokyo, and Manila, and sales executives operating out of 11 other countries.

New York–based Thomson Reuters (which was created in 2008 when Thomson Corporation and Reuters Group merged) is a business intelligence provider that has experienced a lot of change. In 2010, during a substantial reorganization of the business lines with inevitable turmoil, Sisson and key members of his management team focused on creating a mission (in their terms, a *purpose*), set of values (*code of conduct*), and strategic priorities (*direction*) to align and inspire their team. Hence "The Asia Direct Code" was born—a framework for how the team collaborates and delivers business results.

At the heart of the framework is a *teampurpose*. This, says Sisson, is "what motivates us, what fires us up: to be the channel of choice for our customers and staff."

Supporting the purpose is the team code of conduct ("One Code"), which identifies the *values* the team needs to live by, such as courage, openness, focus, and consistent execution. The next level of the framework, called "One Direction," spells out the current *priorities* for the team. Sisson explains, "We focused on a few priorities that we knew would make a material difference to our results. These objectives are established formally in the performance management system. The items currently top of the agenda include growth, people, customer service and retention, and LPIs (Lead Performance Indicators). LPIs include metrics such as sales calls, account reviews, and demos delivered."

While a model like Direct's could remain conceptual, mere words on paper, Sisson and his team drove five key focus areas (as detailed in "One Vision") down to specific tasks, owners, and timeframes.

To make the model stick, it has been communicated, celebrated, and constantly referenced. Progress is formally assessed in quarterly reviews and the model is open to change, as the team always asks, "Is this relevant to us?" There have been some tweaks along the way. For instance, faced with relentless change, Sisson and the team realized they needed to add agility as one of the values in the "One Code."

Part of Sisson's challenge was handling the cultural differences that exist in a team operating across the broader Asia—from Australia to Japan to India. Some terms were avoided because they were too ambiguous. "A concept such as 'respect,' for example, can mean very different things in different contexts," explains Sisson.

"We wanted to make sure there was an element of fun in the model," Sisson continues. An example of this is the introduction of fish or fishing analogies—a topic that resonated across all of the cultures represented on the team. Examples include *The Big Fish* and *Big Pike Day*.

According to Sisson, despite considerable internal change and market uncertainty, his team is now one of the highest performing in Asia and continues to be the highest performing capability of its kind globally. People continue to hold each other accountable to the code. Sisson says, "We didn't realize it at the time, but we actually changed the sales culture of Direct Asia."

Making Alignment Happen

The best practices outlined above might feel like too big an effort if you try to take them on all at once, from a dead start. Surely, your organization has alignment efforts underway already, so you don't have to feel overwhelmed; you just have to feel a sense of urgency. Get your strategy right; communicate and translate it; then build connections to your mission and values if you have them.

Engagement will follow, and you may hear stories within your own organization like this one—the apocryphal tale about the NASA janitor who, when asked what he did, said, "I am putting a man on the moon."

Takeaways

- Maximum contribution cannot occur if employees do not understand what matters to the organization, where they fit in, and how it translates to their daily priorities. Lack of alignment can damage satisfaction, too, as employees fail to find meaning in their work or slip into disengagement when they discover their efforts are misplaced.

- A clear strategy is essential, but a compelling mission and organizational values are valuable tools in driving engagement.

- Ensure that your senior team is in agreement on corporate imperatives, and remember silence does not equal commitment.

- Define a communications approach to reach all employees, and don't rely on one-way messaging; hold leaders accountable for reinforcing organizational imperatives year-round.

- Equip and empower leaders to communicate beyond the facts to capture hearts and minds (because aligned employees don't just know what you need them to do—they act).

- Don't count on your performance management process to effectively align your workforce.

- Encourage dialogue between leaders and employees to translate what matters most to the organization into maximum contribution.

8

Dialogue and Empowerment Trump Action Planning

Don't expect an initiative to do a human's job. Engagement is a personal equation, and as we described in Chapter 4, managers must play a role in helping each employee solve it. Your best managers already understand this, as do many of the leaders we interviewed. They're not waiting for survey data to shape what they do. They don't make engagement a once-a-year priority, distinct from what they do the rest of the time. They always manage their teams with an eye toward results *and* engagement.

How do they do it? Dialogue. Sounds pretty simple: if you manage employees, you need to talk to them. Yet manager-employee conversations are more of a myth than a best practice in a majority of organizations. Many of the managers we interviewed sheepishly acknowledge that they should have more regular sit-downs with their individual team members, but a variety of excuses (e.g., "Not enough time," "Mired in my own work," "Never get around to it") stand in the way. That is too bad, because *dialogue is at the heart of high engagement and sustainable performance.*

So rather than investing your time and resources in driving manager compliance with check-the-box corporate-driven online engagement action plans, get your managers talking to their people.

The Virtuous Cycle: Dialogue, Relationships, and Trust

In Chapter 6 we explored team meetings as a way to act locally on survey findings. Those discussions simultaneously encourage employees to take action to increase their own engagement and create an upward feedback loop that senior leaders can use to spot trends in engagement barriers and levers. Now we're talking about the types of *one-on-one conversations* between managers and employees that should happen all year round.

Trust Matters

Worldwide, 67 percent of all employees who trust their managers are Engaged or Almost Engaged. In contrast, only 28 percent of employees who *do not* trust their managers are Engaged or Almost Engaged. Nearly half of employees who do not trust their managers are actually Disengaged.[1]

These conversations are critical to gathering the type of information managers need to better coach individual employees to higher levels of engagement. But the benefits extend far beyond data gathering. When managers take the time to check in with employees, they demonstrate interest in—and commitment to—their employees' success. The exchange of information that occurs in the conversations strengthens the working relationships and fuels mutual trust.

Johnny Taylor, CEO of the Thurgood Marshall College Fund,[2] speaks of a former boss, Mark Halacy at Blockbuster Entertainment, who understood the power of one-on-one connections. Halacy would have quarterly lunches with his direct reports. He would go beyond just discussing work and inquire what was happening in an individual's personal life. "Mark understood what motivated each employee. It was very cool that he got to know the little things, the personal things. Talking about these things humanized him to me, and me to him."

Taylor's comment underscores the value of managers learning the personal interests and motivators of employees, but research also supports the value of employees getting to know managers as people—beyond their titles and accomplishments. In one study, 87 percent of Engaged employees indicated that they know their manager well or very well compared to less than a quarter of Disengaged workers.[3]

Sharing Information

We are not suggesting that managers become best friends with all their direct reports, socializing off hours or relating detailed accounts of what they did on their days off. Nor is the goal to create unfiltered sharing. (There are clearly differences between authenticity and *authentic leadership*.

London Business School professor Rob Goffee and his colleague Gareth Jones describe this balance as "know and show yourself—*enough*.")[4]

We *are* saying that it's important for managers to share personal motivation and insights about themselves, such as the following:

- What is important to them in their role?
- What challenges are they facing?
- When are they most engaged at work?
- Why did they join this organization and why do they stay?
- What successes or mistakes inform their leadership style?
- When they consider the organization's future, what are they most excited about?
- What is most important to them about the organization's mission, values, or long-term strategy?

Think of your own situation: How well do your team members know you? Do all of them share that knowledge? How can you be sure? Whenever we pose those questions to a group of leaders, we encounter awkward silence or comments such as, "Sure they do. We've been working together for years." But working with people for a long time does not guarantee knowledge of personal motivators.

Go First

When managers share information about their personal motivators, challenges, and engagement drivers, they model the type of open communication they want to create with employees. It creates the climate for a true partnership and a virtuous circle of dialogue, stronger relationships, and increased trust. Managers need to go first. If they don't, the conversations we explore next may fall short of their objectives.

X Marks the Spot

There are at least four types of conversations that your managers can initiate around the playing field of the employee's job—where organizational and individual interests intersect: *performance appraisals, career discussions, onboarding discussions, and engagement reviews*. Each one:

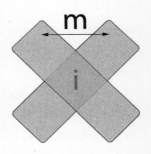

- Plays a specific role in driving employee engagement and business performance.
- Offers a distinct opportunity for managers to approach engagement from a different angle.
- Provides a forum for employees to enlighten their manager about their personal engagement drivers.
- Can be embedded with the language of your organization's engagement model once you have defined it.
- Contains content that should be addressed through *ongoing dialogue*, although it is most often associated with formal, regularly scheduled sit-downs.
- Would be, in an ideal world, driven by your employees as easily as your managers.

Performance Appraisal	Onboarding Discussion
Primary Focus: Maximum Contribution	*Primary Focus: Maximum Contribution*
Provide feedback on results, skills	Exchange information to begin to establish trust
Confirm goals, priorities, expectations	Clarify immediate work priorities, job conditions and requirements
Discuss development for success in current role and upcoming projects	Discuss how to work together effectively
Career Coaching Conversation	**Engagement Review**
Primary Focus: Maximum Satisfaction	*Focus: Maximum Satisfaction and Maximum Contribution*
Help clarify goals, aspirations	Clarify priorities, connection to organization success
Discuss strengths, weaknesses	
Brainstorm growth opportunities, development for future roles, personal goals, networking	Discuss challenges, working relationship, interests/energizers, opportunities to use talents, work environment
	(Insights can inform or shape career and performance discussions)

In theory, three of these conversations are already happening across your organization. If they really are occurring, they are unlikely to be doing enough to support engagement. Let's begin with the most common and most formalized: the performance appraisal.

The Performance Appraisal

This discussion should be on every manager's list already and is likely to be the only conversation that is happening with any consistency or regularity. Unfortunately, it is often seen as an HR-driven task that fills many managers and employees with dread—and does little to actually fuel high performance.

The performance appraisal is primarily about *what employees need to deliver* to drive the organization's success. It's an opportunity to review results, provide feedback on *how* results were achieved (if your performance management systems includes competencies or organizational values), and confirm expectations. It's also the time to talk about any development needed to achieve even greater success in current roles and upcoming projects.

We have seen managers tackle these conversations with a variety of styles—from the meek, conflict-avoidance to the back-of-the-head-with-a-two-by-four. But one thing routinely lacking from performance appraisals is this: how do we build the "success connection"—namely, how do we figure out how best to put your passion and talents to work for the greatest contribution to the organization?

Although performance appraisals appropriately focus on maximum contribution (the *organization's side* of the engagement model), the greatest performance improvement results when an individual's personal motivators, interests, and talents are taken into account.

Yet rarely do performance appraisals address those elements. When they do, they come in at the end of the conversation with a perfunctory question such as, "Where do you want to grow next year?"

Some appraisals run out of time before that topic comes up, and let's be honest: during the performance appraisal your employees aren't thinking about their satisfaction or development. They're waiting to hear answers: What are my ratings or rankings? How much, if anything, will my merit increase be? Have I earned my full bonus?

So rather than trying to reengineer your performance appraisal discussion to tap into personal engagement drivers of employees, we suggest that you make sure

- Your appraisal process drives clarity of priorities and expectations and provides fair and useful performance feedback. (This alone should help move many Honeymooners & Hamsters who have low contribution to a higher engagement level.)

- Your managers understand that performance feedback should be immediate and year-round (even though they're being monitored just once a year).

- You hold your managers accountable for addressing performance problems with clear action steps like performance improvement plans rather than allowing perennial Hamsters or the actively Disengaged to slide by on your payroll with lukewarm ratings.

- Encourage and train your managers to talk with their teams the rest of the year—in career coaching conversations, onboarding discussions, and engagement reviews.

The Career Coaching Conversation

The career coaching conversation is more about *what employees want*. Although it is heavily weighted toward the *individual's side* of the engagement model (maximum satisfaction), career development must happen in the context of the business: your employees' personal aspirations need to be fulfilled while simultaneously addressing organizational needs. You don't really want your employees pursuing *their* career agendas and building *their* skill sets for future employability on *your* payroll without regard to *your* needs, do you? *Career coaching is the perfect opportunity to align your interests with their passion and aspirations.*

Many of the managers we've talked to fear career conversations more than performance appraisals. Worries abound: What is the employee looking for? What jobs are actually available? What if I don't have the answers? How will the team fare if this person takes another job down the hall? The result: conversations don't happen—even in those organizations that boast the common mid-year development/career conversation in their performance management process.

Yet career development is a top reason your employees will leave (the next chapter explores the topic in depth.) For the purposes of this discussion, let's consider the *conversations* that need to take place to help equip employees for a promising, satisfying *future* with your organization.

Career Coaching Tips

The goal of managers in career discussions is to *support* not control. That means it is more important to ask good questions than have all the answers. It's about *helping* employees clarify what they want, build on strengths, address career liabilities, identify development opportunities, network within the organization, and take control of their career success.

Consider your own team. To help them get where they want to be and where your organization needs them to be,

- Consider your organization's strategy, future talent needs, your most pressing team priorities, and the work that needs to be done today. In other words, be crystal clear on what matters most to you and your organization.

- Then consider what you know of each employee's talents, experience, interests, goals, and preferred job conditions.

- Clarify your understanding of their needs during the coaching conversation. Many employees don't really know what they want, so ask questions to get to the motivation behind statements such as "I want P&L accountability," "I want to manage people," or "I want to try something new."

- Help in brainstorming possible matches. Of the work that needs to be done—on your team or elsewhere in the organization—which assignments fit that person's skills and interests?

- Take a breath and relax: not everyone wants *your* job. About half of employees are looking for meaningful or interesting work in their next career move. Only 8 percent want a promotion, and only 14 percent want more money.[5] Those findings support our experience that *successful career coaching conversations often result in changes to the employee's current job scope, not an official change in position*. When you set aside the word *career* and focus on the opportunities for meaningful, interesting work, you will find the possibilities seem endless. After all, there is much work to be done.

Handling Common Career Coaching Challenges

Here are some ideas for handling the trickier career coaching scenarios.

Concern 1: there are no open positions and no obvious future opportunities. First, don't pretend there are any. Together, brainstorm unofficial career development and personal growth in your team member's current job: special projects, stretch assignments, expanded responsibilities, or training. There may also be nontraditional lateral moves to explore. Consider how to raise awareness of this person's strengths and abilities with other leaders by involving him or her in high-visibility presentations and projects. And if the employee can't articulate career or development goals, read on.

Concern 2: the employee desires "career progression" but has no idea what he or she wants. Start by discussing this person's current job satisfaction. It will help the employee understand what to look for in future opportunities. It also sets the stage for reshaping current responsibilities to increase satisfaction and personal growth.

- What aspects of the current role are most satisfying?
- Why does he or she like or not like particular tasks or challenges?
- What talents are underutilized or can be developed further?

Use mind-opening questions to explore ideas for expanding responsibilities and gaining recognition in the employee's current role. It's the employee's career! *As their manager, you don't need to have all the answers.* Encourage the employee to take advantage of organizational resources (e.g., training or online tools) to clarify career aspirations, differentiating talents and drivers of job satisfaction.

Concern 3: You really depend on this employee's contribution to your team and don't want to lose him. Get over it. If your employee is clear about career aspirations and drivers of job satisfaction, he will pursue them with or without you. So be supportive of career conversations. Clarify your understanding of what this person is looking for: A change

(Continued)

in responsibilities to try something new? Development of a certain skill? Experience in leading a project or people? Something to challenge them? Then think about what your team needs to deliver. What projects or tasks can you assign that might satisfy this individual's aspirations? Often, managers can adjust job responsibilities to provide growth opportunities to increase an employee's job satisfaction. This approach is especially useful with less experienced team members because it gives them a relatively safe way to take on responsibilities that they often think they should have (and then find out they dislike). It is also an approach that can take work off your to-do list.

Concern 4: The assignment or role in which the employee is interested may not match her skills or experience. If you and the employee share the same perception of skills and experience, be candid in your belief that there is not a fit. Give specific examples of the employee's skills as well as the requirements of the new role. If your reaction is based on limited information about the role being discussed, suggest that the employee meet with someone who has more hands-on knowledge of the job requirements. Sometimes the issue is timing: you don't believe the employee has been in the current role long enough to acquire critical experience. Be candid about that perception. Don't say, "Wait your turn." Brainstorm ways to build experience more quickly. And remember: *if you are perfectly comfortable recommending a team member for a new role, you've probably waited too long!* Talent management and succession planning involve risk. It's better to encourage and support stretch assignments than lose your top talent.

Concern 5: The employee's perception of talents and weaknesses differs from yours. Keep asking questions to clarify the employee's views. Acknowledge that you don't necessarily agree with those perceptions. Don't turn this conversation into a performance appraisal. Keep the conversation broad with a focus on understanding the employee's perceptions of his talents and weaknesses as well as his aspirations for development and career progression. Then try to find some positive action that you and the employee can take to increase job satisfaction or develop skills in the current job. And if the disconnect in perceptions is significant, schedule a separate, long-overdue conversation to discuss performance.

The Onboarding Discussion

As organizational practices go, onboarding often falls through the cracks. Recruiters source and screen candidates and help land new hires. They may have something to say in orientation sessions. HR generalists often take care of the *Welcome Wagon* activities of orientation: the nuts-and-bolts of getting a new hire introduced to the culture, paired with a buddy and acquainted with employee benefits and personnel policies. Your L&D department might conduct a module on the company's history or provide a short video about the culture and core values. No one owns the process start to finish. Meanwhile, your managers (who are rarely held accountable for formal onboarding) are inclined, as they look to ramp up productivity, to throw new hires into projects, sink or swim, with the message, "The honeymoon is over!"

Yet the honeymoon *isn't over.* On the contrary, it can last half a year. According to a Bersin & Associates research bulletin, estimates of time to full productivity for a new hire range from 8 to

28 weeks, depending on the employee's role.[6] Harvard Business School professor Michael Watkins suggests in his best seller *The First 90 Days* that it takes, on average, 6.2 months for managers in a new role to start adding value to the organization.[7] As Chapter 6 explained, onboarding is an organizational practice that should be aligned with your engagement goals. But as we suggest with career development, you can encourage managers and employees to start talking about the right things while you revise your centralized approach.

Go Slow to Go Fast and Sustain Success

Lorraine Jacomelli, learning and development advisor for global marketing and supply at GlaxoSmithKline in London, stresses that effective onboarding goes beyond the general information addressed in orientation. It aligns employees' day-to-day priorities, which drive maximum contribution. Moreover, she believes that, when done right, onboarding can lay the foundation for continuous re-alignment: "Although work priorities are laid out and discussed clearly and early, business strategy can transform, and with it the work priorities transform. That is why we stress constant communication, especially as things change."

Managers and employees who take the time to have onboarding conversations can accelerate the move from Honeymooner to Engaged and prevent employees with high potential and passion from sliding into Disengagement or just plain failing. They also benefit from getting to know one another and laying the groundwork for an effective working relationship.

The most effective onboarding discussions touch on

- How the employee's job links to the organization's mission and long-term strategy

- The top three priorities the employee needs to accomplish
- A discussion of which skills will be most important in achieving those goals
- What kind of support the employee needs from the manager
- The conditions under which the work needs to get done
- The manager's and employee's work styles and agreements on how to work together effectively

With respect to long-term engagement, the last two points are particularly important. Yet they often are assumed by both parties or discussed in vague terms, which is unfortunate. Misunderstandings of job conditions often result in perceived performance issues and strained working relationships. So the next time you bring a new employee on to your team—or take on a new role yourself—check out the list in the sidebar.

Clarify, Clarify. Then Confirm.

We advise new employees to initiate onboarding conversations and keep asking questions to make sure they really understand what is important to their manager. A manager who says she is hands-off may actually be more of a micromanager than her colleague in the office down the hall. Minimal travel to a manager used to spending time on the road could mean one night a week—which could feel like a lot of travel to an employee used to desk work.

Here are some ideas for talking about job conditions:

- "Talking about my work priorities describes what you need me to accomplish to be successful. Now I'd like

(Continued)

to discuss our work environment to make sure we avoid unnecessary misunderstandings."

- "It sounds like decision making is pretty straightforward, but I'd like to confirm what situations you would like to be involved in."

- "I know you referred to flexible work hours in the interview process. Can you explain a bit more about what you expect and how we all keep each other informed?"

- "How do you see my role in working with . . . ?"

Here are some ideas for talking about working together effectively:

- "What should I know about how you like to work?"

- "How do you like to stay informed?" (e.g., e-mails, phone calls, or in-person meetings; *regularly*, meaning daily, weekly, or monthly check-ins?)

- "How do you like to explore information?" (e.g., brainstorm out loud, on the spot versus listen/read, digest, then share ideas)

- "Do you like more details, or do you like to stay with the big picture?"

- "What is the most important thing I can do to support you?"

- "Can you give me an example of 'too much'?"

- "When you say 'often,' do you mean every day? Every week?"

- *Do not forget to share insights into your own work style but remember you need to flex to accommodate your manager's style.*

The Engagement Review

Let's assume your managers are conducting annual performance appraisals, regular career coaching conversations, and onboarding discussions with their team members.

You may be thinking, "Are engagement reviews really necessary? Especially if my managers conduct team meetings about our annual survey findings?"

Let's face it: you may have talented managers, but they can't read minds. They may have data on their team's engagement levels, but they cannot assume to know who is engaged and who is not. People don't wear brown "I'm a Crash & Burner" labels on their foreheads.

- Employees who are racing around with multiple projects and outrageous deadlines may not be crashing and burning (at least not yet). They may actually be more engaged than ever.
- The chronic complainer may not be totally burnt out or disengaged, just blessed with a critical eye or bad manners.
- The team member who never makes waves and smiles when managers walk by may not actually be satisfied or aligned.

Engagement reviews can avoid dangerous pitfalls that develop when, in everyday interactions, managers make assumptions about their direct reports' engagement levels, and direct reports do not express how they are truly feeling. This communication gap becomes wider as more employees work remotely from their immediate manager or dotted line reports.

Engagement reviews enable your managers to exchange information to ensure that the employees they rely on are connected to your organization's larger purpose, getting what they're looking for at work and applying their unique expertise to carve out a successful future.

Moreover, engagement reviews can shape and improve performance appraisals and career conversations. They reflect a fact-finding approach focused on the employee's *drivers of satisfaction and contribution*. The engagement review *is not* a feedback or targeted coaching session. It *is* the time for managers to discuss topics that will make them more effective coaches and help their employees better manage their own engagement.

Engagement reviews help managers

- Learn or confirm an employee's point of view on job satisfaction and personal success
- Answer questions and provide clarity on what maximum contribution looks like
- Demonstrate support and strengthen their working relationship
- Begin an ongoing dialogue

I think [managers] struggle in grasping the subtleties of the topic—on their role as a manager and how their behavior affects engagement. Policies are a no brainer, but in terms of making engagement something that they live and practice on a day-to-day basis—they struggle. This is why we have to focus on the micro level. When we talk about employees' engagement issues it comes around to managers talking to employees. We role play it and say, "How do you start this conversation off?"
                    —*David Spicer, senior lecturer in organizational change and*
                    head of the Human Resource Management group,
                    Bradford University School of Management, United Kingdom

Timing

Engagement reviews are especially powerful after the team meetings at which engagement survey findings are discussed.

Managers can establish common context and goals when discussing the team's response to survey data, and then use the reviews to discuss individual engagement equations. However, if your organization has not run a survey in the last year, don't wait. Managers and employees can start talking about engagement at any time.

And although a 60- to 90-minute meeting helps ensure a robust discussion, many work environments or large teams may make sit-down conversations impractical. We have found that managers don't actually have to hold formal meetings to learn more about each employee's engagement drivers. If they're walking down the hall with an employee or have 10 minutes for a quick check-in, they can choose one topic to touch on or ask just one question. The first time they do this, the employee may not have an answer. The more often they ask the following questions, the more likely employees will begin to increase self-awareness of what drives their engagement at work—and feel comfortable enough to be candid.

A Flexible Structure

These questions can be asked in a more formal conversation or a less formal check-in. We have grouped them into four categories that won't surprise you if you've read earlier chapters: satisfaction, contribution, talent utilization and development, and working together.

Satisfaction

- What type of assignment energizes you most?
- What do you like most about your job?
- What drags you down?

Contribution

- What questions do you have about how your job fits with the company's current strategy?
- What questions do you have about where you should focus your time and effort?
- What challenges are you facing?

Talent Utilization and Development

- What skills and knowledge would you like to use more?
- Where would you like to grow? Where do you think you need to grow to do your job better?

Working Together

- What ideas do you have for increasing your satisfaction and contribution?
- What do you think you can start doing? Stop doing? Continue doing?
- What would you like me to start doing? Stop doing? Continue doing?

Although the engagement review is primarily a way for managers to gather information, they shouldn't miss the opportunity to *share information and recognize effort*:

- How have organizational and team priorities shifted?
- What opportunities exist for development?
- What special quality or recent accomplishment can you recognize?
- What can you say to personalize your commitment to this employee's engagement?

> ### Remember. . .
>
> As you talk to your own team, remember that you can't have one interaction and check off the box that you've addressed an employee's engagement successfully. Engagement levels are dynamic. Things change. Employees move around the model. This engagement review lays a foundation for specific discussions about performance, development, or career. It also establishes a common language you can use to check in quickly—and regularly—about engagement issues.
>
> The conversation should be ongoing. You'll never be finished talking about engagement—in the same way you're never done discussing how to deliver on the organization's mission and goals.

Moving the Responsibility from Managers to Employees

Until this point we have discussed how managers need to share information about themselves to establish trusting relationships, consistently weave engagement into their daily work conversations, and hold more formal conversations to gather information about their individual team members and fuel engagement.

However, as managers continue to be overwhelmed with competing priorities, you may be reluctant to ask them to take on more. And even those managers who agree wholeheartedly that they should be driving dialogue around engagement may find it hard to manage their priorities to make the time.

Don't forget the I in our engagement model: individuals need to ACT on their own engagement. If you set the expectation that employees are responsible for career success (as we describe in Chapter 9) and provide the training and tools, then employees can drive the career conversations. They may actually choose to solicit advice from colleagues or other managers. And, if they do enlist their manager's support, they'll come in with a discussion plan. Your managers still need to set aside time and focus, but the weight of the conversation is off their shoulders.

The same approach can be taken with onboarding discussions and engagement reviews with the caveats that employees often need more structure and support to confidently and competently drive these discussions, *and* if your managers are really bad, asking employees to take the lead in talking about engagement could result in the type of unfortunate experiences that might send them headed for the door.

The Challenge of Today's Technical Workforce

A common theme in the interviews we have conducted is that highly technical employees and managers don't talk to each other. If they do, these experts (e.g., engineers, scientists, IT professionals, and financial analysts) prefer to talk about the task or project details as opposed to the people stuff that has a profound impact on project success.

So we often hear the question, "How do I get my technical leaders to be people managers, not super-project-managers?" or "How do I convince them that they need to make time for coaching?"

Here are a few tips for encouraging dialogue among more technical workers:

- Provide a structured process and discussion plan for the conversation. Expert employees-turned-managers like to be expert in everything. A detailed road map and thorough planning gives them the confidence to try to talk to their people about engagement.

- Hold them accountable by tracking their activity. Sometimes managers need more of a carrot than a stick to try something they think they won't like. After they conduct one or two meetings, they find the benefits are huge and they'll continue without prompting.

- Support them. Make sure there are experts (in engagement and interpersonal skills) available to field their questions.

- Ask executives to visibly have the conversations you want your leaders to conduct. This tip relates to all managers, not just technical ones. Role modeling can go a long way toward creating more dialogue throughout your organization.

Takeaways

- Relationships fuel engagement and are built on the cornerstones of trust and information sharing.

- Dialogue is about two-way communication. Managers need to share information about themselves to earn trust. And they have to ask questions to understand what each team member needs.

- Don't expect a once-a-year performance appraisal to fuel maximum satisfaction and contribution.

- Encourage employees and managers to have career conversations even when there aren't traditional job openings available. (Read Chapter 9 for more ideas.)

- Encourage regular engagement reviews to get behind survey data and keep the conversation about maximum satisfaction and contribution going.

CHAPTER

9

Career Development

career (intransitive verb): to go at top speed especially in a head-long manner, e.g., a car *careered* off the road.

—*Merriam-Webster Online*

Merriam-Webster's definition may be painfully ironic. Few employees will tell you their careers are going at top speed and seldom does a career go in a headlong direction. Today's careers are more like rudderless ships: stalled, hard to direct, adrift, and at the whims of organizational change. If careers do *career*, it is more a case of abruptly going off the rails. Yet this is neither fulfilling for the individual nor productive for the organization, and it does not have to be this way.

As you map out initiatives in your organization, be aware that *career development is one of the top drivers of engagement and retention.* If employees don't perceive career opportunities and a clear direction within your organization, they will beat a path to the exit.

Yet career development is often dismissed by management for several reasons:

- Employees job hop and don't spend enough time in a company to warrant much attention (or so some leaders assume).
- Ever-evolving technology and changing business plans can make last year's job descriptions obsolete.
- An unstable economy can put current job openings on ice, make them disappear for good, or hold employees hostage (out of fear that the job they have is more secure than a new position elsewhere).
- When budgets are slashed, it is often career initiatives that are first to be eliminated.

As for employees, career (in the broad sense) is high on their list of needs. Two factors consistently top the list of satisfaction drivers for employees in nearly every region in the world and across every engagement level: "career development opportunities and training" and "more opportunities to do what I do best."[1]

At the same time, employees are largely cynical about their employer's attempts to support their careers and disappointed by the resources they receive. For the most part, they believe that they will forge a career *in spite of* their company's policies and procedures.

Why Worry about Career Development?

Engagement and Retention

Many executives we interviewed identify employee engagement and retention as their primary objectives in providing career development support to their employees, with good cause. Prior to 2008 (and the recession that hit much of the globe), only one in two employees believed they had decent career opportunities with their current employer, and over a third expected their next career move would take them elsewhere.[2] Today employees are tired of performing heroics for their employer in a do-more-with-less environment, they're ready to crawl out from the safe place of "at least I have a job," and they're thinking about their future. If you provide career development, it is far more likely your employees will envision their future with you and not with some other organization.

Sustained Organizational Success

Savvy enterprises see a bigger picture: career development is one critical piece in a more complex talent management strategy that often includes succession planning, performance management, redeployment, and targeted development to make sure the organization performs as its markets evolve.

As a leader, you require productivity, innovation, and the right skills in the right place at the right time. To be nimble in the markets you target, your organization must line up top talent to succeed in new roles with short or no learning curves. By providing career development as part of your overall talent management strategy, you increase the chance that your workforce will be willing, ready, and able to move into the roles that you need them to play.

But career development is hard to execute. It's a rocky terrain for the most well-intentioned individuals and organizations. Increasingly elusive definitions of career, the growing need for just-in-time talent management to meet unpredictable market realities, and shifting expectations of the global workforce make it difficult though not impossible for organizations and individuals to align their journeys and achieve their goals together.

It demands a dedicated approach on behalf of your organization and preparedness on behalf of the individual employees.

At the end of the day, *career development is about getting people to where they want to be and where your organization needs them to be.*

What Are Employees Looking For?

As we described in Chapter 1, employees come to work with their own agendas. So *career* is a very personal journey that employees will take with or without your organization. Yet it's likely that the majority of employees in your organization *do not know* what they want their next job to be.[3]

Career may be an even murkier term than engagement for today's workforce because it carries historical connotations and contemporary myths.

If individuals are unclear on their own preference as a next career step, they do not see employers stepping in to assist and guide them: only 23 percent of employees agree or strongly agree with the statement "I know what my employer wants my next job to be." So if there is any difference of opinion and expectations, it is very unlikely that conversations are taking place or any course correction is being applied. In fact, if you ask most employees if they expect their current employer to provide a clear career path for them, the majority (57 percent) will say no. (Younger workers still expect career pathing from their employer, but older workers have learned not to.)

This means that much of today's workforce is drifting, not driven. While this lack of clarity might suit some employees who enjoy the work they now do, it is not a formula for long-term organizational success.

Finally, although the drivers are very personal, when we do explore what is top of mind for employees in their next career move, two big themes stand out:

1. *Personal growth:* Four out of five employees agree that there is nothing wrong with staying in the same job just as long they can try new things to develop their skills.

2. *Promotion is not the goal:* When employees are asked to identify the most important criterion they are looking for in their next position, "Interesting work" (defined as "Work that challenges me, stimulates my intellect or helps me broaden my knowledge or skills") is four times more likely to be picked than "Opportunity for promotion," "Meaningful work." The choices "Work/life balance," and "Financial reward" all rank higher than a promotion opportunity alone.

So what are employees really looking for? Not clarity from their employers, not certainty about their next career step, and not a traditional up-the-ladder promotion, but work that satisfies their desire for personal growth and development. In a nutshell, they are looking for work that works for them.

A Youthful Issue?

Senior leaders frequently express frustration with how younger employees approach their careers. They mention a lack of commitment and a selfish get the skills, get the experience, and get out attitude.

Certainly young people entering the workforce have a different context of employment. We explored this in Chapter 3, and the factors at play also apply to career. Gen Y employees will tell you they want a career, but when you dig deeper, they don't really know what that means specifically, yet have unrealistic expectations of rapid career progression. Certainly the definition as inherited from their parents appears obsolete. They are hoping the organization they work for will help by providing a clear definition and career path they can embrace. But their real challenge is a grasp of their own strengths and skills that they can build upon.

This combination makes it difficult for them to achieve maximum satisfaction or contribution on the job.

But What Are Organizations Doing about Career?

A Barrage of Career Resources

Larger organizations invest substantial effort in career resources. Most employees, when asked, admit to having access to 11 of the 15 most-common career tools deployed by organizations (especially the larger ones). These include (in order of frequency) job postings, training/workshops, descriptions of job levels/grades/responsibilities, criteria for advancement, development planning assessments, online information… the list goes on.

Beyond these common stand-alone resources, some companies really go to town: they use a unique blend of components, reflecting their industry, workforce population, organization culture, size, and most-pressing business issues. The most-ambitious initiatives are organization-wide and top-down, containing internal marketing strategies, competency models, profiles of nontraditional career paths, and training and tools for employees at all levels.

Employees in large organizations are bombarded with career resources. Still, many leaders express frustration that their organizations receive low marks for career opportunities on employee surveys. So why the disconnect?

Only a quarter of employees agree that their career aspirations are supported with a talent management system or initiative. The vast majority believe they have not personally benefited from the career resources their organizations have provided.

Clearly, tackling career is far more complex than providing career paths or more jobs. In fact, most stand-alone online tools, libraries, or communities result in little use and even less perception of value.

But It Is Clarity That Is Required

Most employees do not have clarity around their career aspirations or drivers of job satisfaction. That is their problem, not their employer's—until they leave to pursue a vague, often unfounded notion of a promising career move. Being given a broader range of options is not the answer when we do not know what criteria to apply to make a selection. We need a different approach. Here is how one organization approached the challenge of addressing career.

The Razorfish Story

In 2009, executives at the digital advertising agency Razorfish noticed a troubling trend. During exit interviews, soon-to-be-former employees complained that their main reason for leaving was that they didn't foresee good career opportunities in front of them. In its biannual engagement survey, employees seemed to be unsettled and drifting, according to Dee Fischer, the company's director of organizational development.

Razorfish had been acquired twice in two years: first by Microsoft in 2007 and then in 2009 by Publicis, the multinational communications giant. The company went from being a fast-moving and nimble organization to being part of two global titans that had stricter rules and bigger bureaucracies. The global recession was also contributing to a sense of company-wide unease.

It became apparent to Fischer and her colleagues that they needed to refocus on career development as part of an engagement plan that would change employee perceptions and help retain top talent.

In September 2010, Fischer and her Razorfish colleagues conducted the company's first annual Career Month. It provided employees with access to thought leaders, career-related learning opportunities, cross-discipline networking, and an online CareerLab portal. Career Month was designed as a high-visibility launch of ongoing tools and activities that would facilitate career progression year-round.

Razorfish executives wanted career month to be a time for employees to begin having one-on-one conversations with their managers about coaching and mentoring opportunities and to document their career progression from entry level to senior status executives.

"We want our employees to take charge of their own careers, to put the pieces together for themselves and carve a unique path," says Fischer. "Creative, unique careers don't always match hierarchical descriptions."

That first Career Month kicked off with author Daniel Pink, who delivered a motivational in-person presentation in Chicago that was simulcast to all the company offices and remote locations. Pink's message was based on his book *The Adventures of Johnny Bunko: The Last Career Guide You'll Ever Need*, and was a call to action for individual employees to own—and take action on—their careers.

Today the CareerLab portal is a 24/7 resource where employees go to get career management advice, access development tools, and find networking tips. Yet Razorfish views its online tools as secondary to employees establishing real-life coaching relationship with their managers or other senior executives who can assist them with their internal career plans.

"Conversation trumps information," Fischer insists. "Listening to you, honoring where you're coming from is a huge engagement driver. Ultimately the experience of having a conversation about career is good and in itself can be re-engaging."

The company also deploys mentors using a specific philosophy based on open communication:

> Mentoring is not formalized. We have an open culture where someone doesn't have to fear asking if I can have a conversation with you about mentoring. We want it to evolve informally. It has to have an emotional resonance that sometimes you can't force.

Finally, career at Razorfish goes even further than the company itself: employees have the opportunity to move within the larger umbrella of a corporation. Razorfish is part of Vivaki, a sub-brand of media giant Publicis Groupe. Razorfish employees have job opportunities at other digital advertising companies in the Vivaki group, such as Starcomm and Digitas.

"We're working with different agencies for short term assignments," Dee Fischer says. "We can transfer you to another company within the family."

Redefining *Career*

Believe it or not, it is good news that the majority of employees don't expect your organization to provide clear career paths. How could you? As the organization morphs to keep up with the demands of today's global economy, most routes are likely to be redrawn as fast as you map them out. Job descriptions are out of date before the drafts are finalized.

And yet too often employees still perceive *internal* career as something that is going to be presented to them on a platter by managers—a tap on the shoulder and a clearly defined job description for the next role. This expectation needs to be changed.

As traditional career ladders (shaped by organizations and climbed steadily by company men and women) disappear, it becomes important for organizations to help define the primary guideposts that individuals should use to redefine and navigate today's uncharted career landscape. Employees who are truly striving to achieve full engagement for their own sake would ideally stop looking to a new employer and start developing a personal career path or series of projects internally, in line with the company's shifting priorities.

One-size-fits-all career approaches are rapidly becoming redundant as employees expect the same personalized experience in their careers that they get as consumers. So kill off old notions of career, and earn the commitment of the workforce to a future of meaningful work and mutual success.

The bottom line: if employees understand what matters to them, what they can offer, and where they can make a difference for their employer, they will be better able to make the right choices—and also position themselves as the right people to get the work done.

Today's Career: A Journey, Not a Destination

To start the conversation on redefining career, it helps to use a simple analogy, as suggested by Ed Lawler, professor of business at University of Southern California's Marshall School of Business:

> In the past, choosing a career was like buying a one-way train ticket from Rome to Copenhagen on a local train that made all the stops along the way. . . . Today choosing a career is more like buying a lifelong Eurailpass, with no set final destination, no fixed travel agenda, and no timetable.[4]

The key takeaway from Lawler's analogy? You cannot take anything for granted when it comes to your career. There are no preestablished career routes; there is only a wide-open network of options, and you can take your career down any one of them, at your own speed.

The foundation for employees' future career success is an understanding of their engagement drivers and the capabilities they have to move the organization's strategy forward. It continues with a plan to explore and take action on both the obvious—and not so obvious—opportunities for development or challenging work. Sometimes the best career move is a subtle change in the current job.

When employees see career as encompassing lateral moves, skill development, stretch assignments, and special projects—not just promotions or advancement—they will find more satisfying opportunities with you, their current employer. If you provide an exciting journey, people will stop wondering about what stops are called along the way.

Three Cornerstones

As with engagement, career development in an organization needs to be a two-way street with employers and employees working in unison to explore what organizational opportunities exist, and how your employees can get from point A to point B. This again means shared responsibility. An employee needs to take control of her own career prospects. This remains a tricky task (if not impossible) if that employee doesn't know what direction she is heading in.

This is where a good executive or manager is most critical. Keeping your people from leaving an organization isn't always about more money or even a promotion. People want new experiences, special projects, and the promise of exciting work in the future. Increasingly, employees want to find ways of balancing their work and personal life, and their manager is instrumental in that process.

So start by establishing three cornerstones of career development success:

1. *Individuals must own their careers*, be clear about what they're looking for, and be committed to taking action.

   - Know yourself: Develop an understanding of engagement drivers and capabilities.

   - Know your options: Explore the obvious—and not so obvious—opportunities for development or challenging work.

   - Take action: Career does not start with the role change. It starts with acquiring the skills, building the relationships, and laying the foundation in order to progress to that next role.

2. The organization must *have a point of view about career development* and provide tools and a structure that allows employees to develop in their careers in the context of what the organization needs.

3. *Managers stand at the crossroads* where their team members' capabilities and goals meet the organization's priorities. They need to understand and buy in to the organization's career development point of view. They also must be competent and confident in supporting (not directing) employees' career journeys. It is the role of your managers to help employees realistically align their aspirations with the organization's goals.

Which brings us to the first hurdle: managers find career conversations very challenging.

The Challenges of Career Coaching and Mentoring

Mixed Manager Competence   Many managers are often afraid to have the career conversation or to discuss career plans and opportunities with their direct reports. While many managers may not like performance appraisals, they at least feel that they're able to maintain some kind of control over that process.

It's an entirely different matter when it comes to career coaching.

The role of career coach is typically thrust on managers. As a result, they never have the types of discussions about career development and goals that an objective career coach would, and sometimes for good reason. If a manager tells his best employee about great opportunities available on another manager's team, he could lose that employee. "What if the employee is actually really after my job," a manager might think. As for objectively advising a direct report on opportunities outside the company, forget it.

Managers can be skeptical or even fearful if they are not involved in career development, especially if their own past career experience has not been positive. Still, managers should be trained and available to be career coaches and should not abdicate that role. You should build managers' buy-in to your career approach. Make sure that they're not excluded from the process.

Capitalize on the position that managers hold since they should already be having performance and development conversations with their teams. Encourage them to add career to the mix. They don't need to have all the answers.

"Some managers gravitate to coaching, [whereas] others are freaked out by it," says Fischer of Razorfish. "There can be a basic resistance. We want them to feel confident, so we're offering career coaching for managers once or twice a year."

Talent Hoarding

How do you convince a manager to let go of one of her top-performing team members? Can managers really be expected to trade in the feel-good factor of helping a direct report progress for the headaches of retraining and rehiring someone new?

Talent hoarding presents a specific challenge to organizations. If trapped too long and passed over for well-deserved opportunities, top performers will eventually leave.

Certainly managers may be unintentionally hoarding talent, or doing so out of necessity. During a hiring freeze or bad economy, there may be no opportunity to replace a key performer who is snatched up by another department.

A 2012 report[5] examined job stagnation in the U.S. government's Senior Executive Service (SES) agency. The SES was established in 1978 and intended to rotate executives through different government agencies. The goal was to allow top talent to circulate freely among agencies and ultimately promote a more effective government.

The report found that this has not happened. Instead, the agencies have hoarded much of their senior talent: "Almost half of the U.S. government's 7,100 senior executives have stayed in the same position in the same organization their entire SES career. A mere 8 percent have worked at more than one agency during their SES tenure."

This kind of hoarding behavior is also common in the private sector.

This was a challenge at retail firm Landmark. "Career progression at Landmark was very formal. Managers were tasked with directly identifying people for promotion. We have tried to make this process more flexible so that people can show the initiative without waiting to be picked out by their superiors."

The first step in this process was LaunchPad, and internal job posting site that provided an opportunity for any employee to apply for an opening. If an employee is successful in their application, HR will then double back with his or her manager to ease the transition.

"We found this to be a great initiative because previously managers were not always willing to let go of their top performers," says B. Venkataramana, the India senior VP and chief people officer.

By addressing managers who hoard talent, giving individuals the opportunity to rotate into different positions and take stretch assignments, you can increase the chance of keeping high performers happy within the organization for many years to come. In the eight months prior to our conversation, 420 people (or 4 percent) of the employees had moved across divisions within Landmark. An additional 50 people had moved from India to the Gulf region.

Go (Cautiously) Beyond Managers   But it can also be a good idea for you to bring in help from outside or use internal coaching resources, if you believe your employees can benefit. You should consider internal or external career coaches and to supplement the manager's role, internal HR consultants, peer coaching, and/ or senior level mentoring can be used.

Sometimes, however, bringing in external coaches can backfire if the fit between the coaches and the staff isn't right. Dee Fischer recalls that several years ago, Razorfish brought in career coaches to meet with high potential employees at one of their

Career Month events: "The coaches didn't culturally resonate with the employees," she says. "They were competent coaches but there wasn't a generational trust."

Fischer says that there was a clash between the button-downed middle-age coaches, and the casually dressed Razorfish employees who are mostly in their 20s and 30s.

Mentors   In some organizations a formalized mentoring program can work extremely well as a career development tool, while informal arrangements can also be successful. The better approach will be the one most in line with your organization's culture.

Alexis Fink, the director of talent management infrastructure at Microsoft Corp, says the company has had great success with its internal mentoring program that not only pairs junior employees with senior managers, but also supports peer mentoring. "There are expectations that senior executives will mentor high potentials," Fink says. "We use self-selected mentors that are self-sustaining. Helping other people is an important part of the culture. A rising tide lifts all boats."

Mentoring has another benefit—one that is useful in selling Mentoring to managers: "It allows you to build on relationships. People tend to get different jobs every few years. So your peers and collaborators might one day be your direct reports or you might be working for them."

Mentoring helps in understanding company politics, building your network, and exploring opportunities for career moves that may not be obvious to your manager.

On the flip side, Johnny Taylor, of the Thurgood Marshall College Fund, remembers how being a mentor to a direct report backfired.

When he was an HR executive at Paramount Studios, Taylor agreed to mentor a subordinate who had approached him about serving in that capacity. Soon after, the relationship went sour. The mentee applied for an open position in the department that Taylor was hiring for, but did not get the job. Taylor believed that another applicant was better qualified. "That person still will not speak to me over the incident," he recalls. "I should never have agreed to be their mentor."

In conclusion, mentoring can be an effective approach, but it requires some supervision. You will need the right chemistry, the right fit between mentor and mentee. Mentors and mentees also need to be trained and expectations need to be clear on roles and scope of support. Mentors should not be relied on to provide career support if a manager is falling short—you may find employees turning to mentors to do an end run around their manager.

Recommendations

We mentioned at the beginning of this chapter that career is not easy for the organization to crack. It takes concerted effort and involves many moving parts. But we do have a list of 14 recommendations we like to use when reviewing career efforts inside organizations. We hope it will provide you with a good frame of reference as you review your own career efforts.

1. *Redefine career first*. Make sure career is addressed in your engagement strategy. Focus on defining your organization's career philosophy rather than defined career channels.

   Since individuals' perceptions of career vary, define the term for your organization. What does "career" look like in this organization? What's your organization's career philosophy? Who plays what roles? What different paths have individuals taken to achieve their goals?

2. *Beware the* career *word.* The next time employees express dissatisfaction about career opportunities (for example, as an item in a survey), take the time to discover the need behind the need. It may not be a clear path, raise, new title, or their boss's job. It may be new challenges, flexibility, or skill development.

3. *Link career development and business priorities.* Employees must understand the organization's long-term strategy and what is required of the workforce to execute it. The more employees know and care about the organization's direction and business priorities, the more willing and able they'll be to satisfy their career aspirations and apply the necessary skills when the organization needs them. This ties back to alignment as discussed in Chapter 7.

4. *Identify the work required to drive organizational success.* Our findings suggest that most employees care about the work itself—how it challenges them, provides meaning, and fits into their personal lives. The goal, then, is to help employees find the work they want to do and make sure it's the very work that will move your organization forward.

5. *Help employees clarify what they want.* If employees don't know what they want, they won't know when they've got it. That's not the organization's problem—unless the organization is trying to align employee interests and skills with its business strategy. The more you can help employees become clear on their personal values and goals, the greater the chance that they can pair their aspirations with your requirements. Employees shouldn't be left on their own to figure this out. They are ultimately responsible for their career success but often are paralyzed by their choices. And you don't want free agents focused solely on personal goals.

6. *Build managers' buy-in and skills.* Whereas managers should not drive career development initiatives, they can certainly derail them if they're not part of the process. The executives we interviewed described managers as skeptical, sometimes fearful, and even prone to "disinheriting their staff" if they did not have an active role or have the chance to buy-in to career development efforts from the start. Don't exclude them.

7. *Managers must be confident and competent at talking about career.* They should know individual employees' abilities and interests, and they should have a sense of where the organization is going and what skills will be required in the future. This positions them well as career coaches. Yet they carry a lot of fears and misconceptions that need to be addressed before they can effectively facilitate employees' career journeys. And they have to be ready for a wide variety of employee situations. Give managers the opportunity to address these concerns and practice the skills in a safe environment and not on their own staff. We covered the manager's challenges and conversation tips in Chapter 8.

8. *Put conversation above information.* Employees don't find online resources, printed brochures, and other information sources particularly valuable. When they talk about major career influences, they mention career coaches, former managers or mentors, networks of colleagues, even training sessions—where they have exchanged ideas and gotten advice.

   Capitalize on the position that managers hold since they should already be having performance and development conversations with their teams. Encourage them to add career to the mix. They don't need to have all the answers. Provide guidance on what you expect them to do or not do.

Online or printed information (such as alternative career paths, profiles of successful career navigators, or tips on interviewing) best play a role as support resources, not the primary component of successful career development initiatives.

9. *Take a multifaceted approach.* No one tool or resource will scratch every employee's itch and drive the organization's performance. Therefore you need to approach career development as part of a strategic talent management strategy, with a blend of information, high-tech tools, coaching, development, and HR processes.

It is not enough to just present the option of an online career tool. Nor is it enough to provide just career coaching and mentoring. But if you can take multiple approaches, with comprehensive feedback and follow-up, you will be building a career development plan that drives engagement and will serve you and your employees well in the years to come.

Evidence that these efforts pay off: companies that embrace this approach see a nearly 50 percent reduction in turnover,[6] a significant increase in lateral moves, more effective employee-manager partnerships, positive employee feedback, and smoother succession planning sessions.

For example, Microsoft offers its employees career development days, self-discovery exercises, and enormous online resource tools. "We have a tool that's basically a Cliff Notes version of every job in the company where you can compare jobs side by side, like stoves at Home Depot," Fink says.

But Microsoft also encourages informational interviews with managers and other employees, an opportunity to find out what an individual's job entails.

10. *Encourage cross-functional experience, education, and networking.* Organizations promote lateral moves, but they aren't easy to pull off. To smooth the way, successful organizations use temporary assignments, cross-functional development initiatives, and employee affinity/networking groups. Online networking works well in one financial institution—but it was instituted after employees established strong personal relationships face-to-face in a high-potential training session.

Some people are hungry for international experience. Before we were not set up to facilitate this. But we realized that it was a crazy situation: we had agencies recruiting Indian talent for our Middle East operations. Guess where these agencies recruited most of their candidates? Right here from Landmark's own India staff! So providing an internal channel for these candidates was a no-brainer.

—*B. Venkataramana, Landmark Group*

11. *Consider internal or external career coaches.* Our interviews and survey data underscore the usefulness of solid career advice. One bank opted for senior-level mentors because HR was not well positioned to make important introductions to line executives; other organizations look to HR to play the role of career coaches. Some are experimenting with external consultants. Why not rely exclusively on managers, who are often in the best position to coach? Availability, skill level, even perceptions come into play. One interviewee from the United Kingdom explained, "My manager also needs to look after his own interests, and the two [his career and mine] may sometimes conflict."

12. *Get them early: onboarding/induction.* Revisit your onboarding process and make sure the career approach and philosophy is clearly articulated.

Alexis Fink of Microsoft says that the company focuses on "onboarding" and preparing workers for success: "We spend a lot of time with brand new hires in the first one to six months, finding out their career goals and putting them on the right job path."

13. *Don't forget skill development.* Realistically, employees can't successfully navigate their careers and meet your organization's evolving needs without expanding their skill sets. Sometimes those goals can be reached without a change in jobs.

14. *Take a reality check.* Nearly three-quarters of our survey respondents indicated that their organization's career resources aren't helpful. What about yours? Ask your employees about their careers—and the tools you provide. What are they looking for? What resources are most valuable? What barriers exist to pursue their goals within your organization?

Juniper Networks: The Art of Lateral Moves

Juniper Networks, a Silicon Valley–based manufacturer of high-speed switching routers with 9,000 employees worldwide, is a good example of a company that has begun to help its employees redefine their notions of career.

Colleagues (Juniper does not call their workers employees) are encouraged to consider careers as more than just linear paths. While many organizations only celebrate promotions, Juniper helps people grow their portfolio of skills and experience through lateral moves.

This approach is essential for organizations with expert professionals including technologists, engineers, and scientists. Steve Dolan, senior director of Leadership and Organizational Effectiveness at Juniper Networks, references research that says that technical professionals exhibit six primary needs:[7]

1. Autonomy

2. Achievement

3. Keeping Current

4. Professional Identification

5. Participation in Mission and Goals

6. Collegial Support and Sharing

Parts of the career development challenges facing Juniper were similar to those at Razorfish. The company was finding that there was too much voluntary attrition. In exit interviews, they learned that people were leaving because they wanted to grow their capabilities and careers. Those who were staying and advancing to management positions were doing so for the wrong reasons: based on their technical prowess and not necessarily their interest or aptitude for management positions.

"We revised our career architecture so that we have a dual career ladder: a management path for individuals interested in pursuing people management, and a professional path for individuals who want to deepen their expertise as technical or functional experts," says Dolan.

Dolan adds that Juniper's career architecture doesn't compel people to choose a managerial track in their career development but reinforces the notion that colleagues can migrate between the two paths, as well as moving up.

Juniper trains its managers to support individual ownership of their careers. The company also creates a curriculum that teaches managers ways to develop skills that allow conversations with colleagues about their careers.

Managers will meet periodically with their direct reports to discuss career aspirations.

"Engineers like to talk about projects, not the X (model of engagement) or career. We need to increase their comfort level in discussing aspirations, not just tasks," Dolan says.

Juniper has created growth and career planning program tools and has virtually changed their entire philosophy about traditional career development. Growth and career planning are now part of the evaluation process. Rating and rankings (considered polarizing) have largely been eliminated. Appraisals have been eliminated and replaced by two annual conversation days that are tied to the company bonus/compensation system. These conversations are a two-way street in which colleagues can provide feedback to their managers. The company also provides its people with an online set of career development tools and resources called Ispark.

"We talk about career not as a 'P' (Promotion) but about lateral moves, growing in current roles and new experiences," says Dolan. "Each colleague is responsible for his or her own career. . . . The manager supports and creates the environment for doing the best work possible."

Juniper uses a new system for evaluating talent called Talent Matters, which allows management to assess if colleagues are currently aligned with the company—and if they might be aligned with the organization in the future. They evaluate colleague contributions, goals, and how they get things done.

Rotations

Innovative companies throughout the world are taking career development in interesting directions through stretch assignments and short-term positions/rotations that allow employees to develop new skills and new opportunities while advancing the goals of the organization.

Tony Ling, VP, human resources, at Dianping.com, explains how this dot-com uses six-month job rotations to develop employees, sustain culture and progress strategy:

When we are going to develop a new market, it would be tempting to purchase a local competitor. But instead, we approach our top salespeople in Shanghai, and offer them a six-month rotation to go and open the new Dianping office. This provides them with a development opportunity. They hire the local sales team, infuse the Dianping culture, coach, and develop them. We refer to these assignments as our "pioneering team."

After six months, Dianping provides local career mobility by promoting the best local talent into the office management role.

But as Awdhesh Krishna, managing director and global head of HR wholesale corporate at Nomura Bank, explains, functional stereotyping puts limits on an organization's willingness to do rotations:

We don't take risks on people as much as we should, and we pay the price in terms of our leadership pipeline. This is a big challenge in banks, but equally so in pharmaceutical firms where the top executives often come from a pure R&D background or in the oil industry with engineering heads who have little experience in other functions. To be an effective leader you need exposure throughout your career to all the different functions of the organization. Developing that pipeline is all about betting on people. You have to make job rotation a part of the culture.

The challenge is not just with the organization's practice. It's also about the individual's expectations. We find that for the first 10 years of their career people are dying to get cross-functional experience and the exposure they might gain through job rotations. After that they have built such a comfort zone, they become hypnotized.

Stretch Assignments

Steve Miranda of Cornell believes that high potentials especially should be nurtured through short-term assignments allotted with an eye on the long run. You should explain to employees how these brief opportunities will benefit their long-term careers.

Miranda says that it helps to put people on projects that push their limits and teaches them new skills: "Everything new that you do should stretch you, but not break you." A person with strong analytical skills, but weak on finance, could be assigned to a project that can bolster his financial acumen and help him develop as an employee (assuming financial literacy is a requirement for the long-term career goal).

"Sometimes bosses know what will help in your progress," Miranda says. "Every short-term initiative should be positioned with a longer term goal."

Alexis Fink, of Microsoft, says the company offers stretch assignments for employees in which they are offered the opportunity to temporarily try stints at new positions. For example, if one employee goes on parental leave, another could be tapped to take on that job, from a different department.

"It's like, try this job on for size," says Fink. "Stretch assignments can build a resume and let someone take another path, if they are interested in moving in a new direction. It's an opportunity to date a job, without having to get married."

Takeaways

1. It is in the organization's best interests to have a strong handle on the topic of career.
2. While organizations provide a wide array of career information, it's actually clarity that is the biggest hurdle for individuals.

3. To be effective, organizations first have to dispel outdated notions of career.

4. Employees must own their own career but organizations should help employees clarify what they want.

5. Organizations must take a multifaceted approach but make sure the conversations between employee and manager take center stage.

6. Managers should be trained to coach employees. It can also be extremely useful to utilize internal or external career coaches, and to supplement the manager's role with internal HR consultants, peer coaching, and/or senior-level mentoring.

7. Growing in place, or lateral moves, can be just as valuable as promotions if they offer opportunities for learning new skills.

CHAPTER

10

Measuring ROI

Not everything that counts can be measured. Not everything that can be measured counts.

—*Albert Einstein*

When it comes to measuring the specific cause-and-effect relationship between higher engagement and business results, ask yourself a question: Do you need to be convinced?

There are plenty of studies that make the business case for engagement by linking earnings per share (EPS), productivity, discretionary effort, innovation, customer loyalty, and quality. Among our favorites are

- James Heskett, "Putting the Service Profit Chain to Work," *Harvard Business Review*, 2008. "The impact of satisfied and productive employees is 'astronomical' on increasing the lifetime value of a loyal customer, especially when referrals are added to the economics of customer retention and repeat purchases of related products."

- Alex Edmans, "Does the Stock Market Fully Value Intangibles? Employee Satisfaction and Equity Prices" (paper), Wharton School, University of Pennsylvania, 2010. An analysis of the best companies to work for in America indicated that "high levels of employee satisfaction generate superior long-horizon returns."

- Hewitt Associates. In 2009, high-engagement firms had total shareholder return that was 19 percent higher than average. In low-engagement organizations, total shareholder return was actually 44 percent below average.

Measuring employee engagement is relatively easy; measuring the *direct contribution* of increased engagement to your enterprise's financial results is complicated, unreliable, and time-consuming. Many executives from around the world accept that engagement is important, and yet acknowledge the complexity of its causal relationship to business success. Daniel Sarkadi, the sales director of Generali-Providencia, one of Hungary's largest insurance companies, says,

> Engagement does strongly correlate with profitability. In my understanding, business is too complex a story just to measure the effect of one factor influencing the whole. But if the engagement issue is managed consciously and aligned and integrated with other prior development processes, we will soon see the revenue-generating results.

If the ROI of engagement seems obvious to you, then skip to the next chapter. But if you need to go down the ROI path, then we have some things to cover.

Engagement at Sea and on Shore

Before we get into the details of ROI, let's consider one organization where the issue of correlative versus causative articulated particularly well: Royal Caribbean Cruises Ltd. (RCCL). According to Barbara Kallay, vice president, Human Resources Business Support, and Jay Rombach, associate vice president, Human Resources for Celebrity Cruises (one of Royal Caribbean's subsidiaries), this company has developed a sophisticated employee engagement strategy, including tracking employee engagement against financial performance and guest satisfaction. This example illustrates how the ROI dynamics differ from shipside (staff working on Celebrity Cruises' ships) and shoreside (the corporate and support functions such as IT, bookings, finance, and marketing):

Shipside: Rombach explains, "We've tracked engagement data and guest satisfaction results for the last three years and we've been able to show a steady increase in employee engagement on ships. Guest satisfaction has also increased, following the same pattern. There's definitely a *correlation*. We know there are other factors at play in guest satisfaction—we have new ships, for example, which have a positive impact. We've been flat on employee turnover as well. But we *believe* our engagement efforts have made a huge difference."

Shoreside: Kallay counters, "Corporate is less metrics driven overall, which presents more of a challenge for us. Shoreside engagement scores went up in 2011 over 2010. But correlations between engagement scores and business outcomes have been harder to identify [than connections shipside]. They are less direct. This is our opportunity to improve moving forward. We plan to look at the connections department by department. Some functions are naturally easier to track. Inbound phone sales, responding to the website 'book a cruise now' link, is a good example. We can correlate higher employee engagement scores with higher sales and lower turnover. But we want to make those connections across the enterprise."

RCCL's experience highlights several key takeaways that we will come back to:

1. While employee engagement contributes to business results, other factors also have an impact. Extrapolating the various factors can be challenging.

2. The way that you will assess ROI—the metrics you use to monitor progress—will depend on the nature of that business or department. No point tracking the ROI of engagement in the internal IT group based on sales; the number of help desk tickets dealt with or internal client satisfaction is a much better measure.

3. The relationship between engagement levels and business outcomes will be more evident in some parts of the business than in others. This does not mean that engagement is less important, but its contribution to results may be less explicit.

Quid Pro Quo

Ideally, if we were to measure ROI, we would have a nice quid pro quo model, a direct relationship between investment in engagement efforts and bottom line returns. We invest x and our profit goes up y. If x is smaller than y, we scale up.

So what we need is a clear line of sight between changes in engagement levels and business outcomes such as higher sales, higher productivity, higher profitability, or higher customer satisfaction.

We have instruments for measuring engagement levels. With a well-designed survey and research process, we can measure and monitor engagement levels across the organization. We can easily assess both the hard costs (consultants, training costs, systems investments) and the soft costs (management time, time spent training) of running engagement initiatives. The next step is to determine how we connect the engagement scores to the business outcomes.

Let's consider for a minute the chain of events involved in the enterprise's value creation process. For this, we can borrow Kaplan and Norton's balanced scorecard strategy map.[1] Figure 10.1 is a sample mapping of the chain of events that go into creating that bottom line impact and the ultimate prize of shareholder value.

This helps illustrate how many steps and factors sit between the motivated and prepared workforce, seen under "Organizational Capital" at the bottom-right side of the chart, and the financial metrics we so closely monitor, seen at the top. This diagram helps people appreciate the steps, processes, and interactions that occur between changes in engagement and measurable financial results.

It is possible that an exact ROI study can be done. But you would need to have a handle on all those other variables to be able to determine the specific contribution of engagement to the overall financial results, accounting for all other changes across the system.

Dr. David Spicer, senior lecturer in organizational change, teaches MBA-level classes at Bradford University School of Management in the United Kingdom. He sees firsthand how a wide range of leaders from different industries approach engagement:

[When it comes to ROI] you have to ask yourself "what is the actual relationship between the greater motivation of

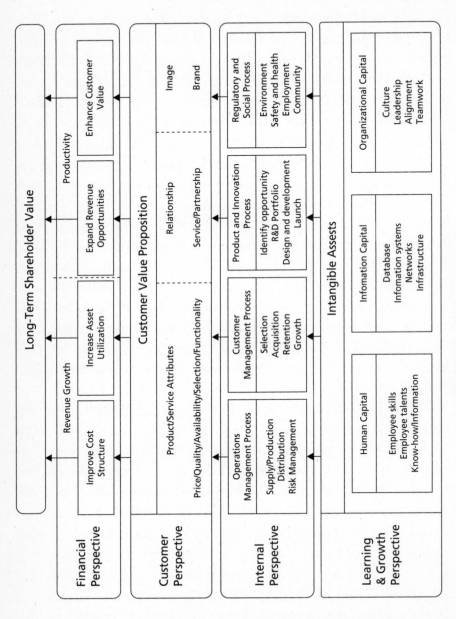

FIGURE 10.1 Sample Mapping

an employee and the organizational outcomes?" There is a long chain of steps between those two. Higher engagement will lead to more persistence and effort which should result in greater individual performance. Under the right circumstances this will increase department performance. People looking for direct ROI are looking at bad math. Engagement is part of a whole set of factors and you can't separate it out from other initiatives.

Employee Retention

We find that the first port of call for many ROI studies is to track a relatively easy business metric such as retention. Engaged employees will remain with the organization; therefore, high engagement saves you money through lower turnover, re-hiring, and training.

The fact that your employees stay does not mean they are engaged, however. (They could be Hamsters or the Disengaged!) You might even want some employees to leave, a process of "productive attrition" that in the long term would improve your overall performance.

Besides, even the Engaged or Almost Engaged leave. In industries where competition for talent is fierce, we have seen engaged employees jump ship because the attractions of higher salaries or perks were simply too tempting. In these cases, you are dealing with "regretful turnover," but not disengagement.

Not Employee Retention

If turnover is not a particularly useful metric, what else can you draw a line of sight to? Ideally, you would be measuring performance, but in most work situations it is difficult to link the increased engagement of one individual, team, or division to long-term business improvement.

The challenges of drawing a straight line cause-and-effect between heightened engagement and business outcomes are fourfold:

First: there are many other factors at play in any one organization, so drawing a direct cause-and-effect relationship (positive or negative) is challenging. Even where your model is accurate, it is tricky identifying the contribution of a single factor to specific business results.

Second: what may at first glance appear to be a reliable indicator of engagement isn't necessarily reliable, and may have many other factors influencing it. A classic example is the cars in the car park metric. The small number of cars left in the company parking lot after 6:00 P.M. can be indicative of the growing prevalence of flextime and telecommuting. Many people's cars could be parked in front of their house but they themselves still be connected and working.

Third: the outcomes you want are different from other companies. The return you are chasing could be something entirely different from that of even your direct competitor. So the straight line cause-and-effect you read about in that Harvard Business Press article may not translate to your work setting.

Fourth: The tools at our disposal for measuring engagement are in themselves subject to bias and variance between samples.

Beware the Hawthorne Effect

Executives need to be aware of the implications of tracking any data in the organization. As the Hawthorne

studies from the 1920s proved, the simple act of paying attention to a given metric can drive behavior. The
resulting behavior change may be positive or negative,
but the score or the metric is not the prize. And as soon
as the measurement process ends, behaviors return to
old patterns.

So we address these challenges by building a measurement
methodology that takes a longitudinal approach and tracks indicators, not a direct causal relationship:

Step 1: Make sure that you are crystal clear on the purpose
of driving engagement in your enterprise. What are the
outcomes you are chasing? We recommend writing an
Engagement Vision Statement—a clarifying description of why engagement is important in achieving your
business outcomes, and what you believe will be visibly
different as a result of heightened levels of individual
engagement.

Step 2: Build a dashboard of business metrics that you would
expect to trend along with engagement, based on the
outputs that you are looking for. These may be existing
metrics in your Balanced Scorecard approach, but may
also be reports on existing data that is currently ignored or
new data-gathering exercises.

Your primary focus has to be the development of a reliable
dashboard that allows you to track *progress over time* and not a
direct ROI measurement.

Employee Engagement and the Balanced Scorecard

Most business leaders we have worked with will mentally compartmentalize (and study somewhat separately) four sets of metrics:

1. The first (and most likely to get attention) are the *hard business metrics, typically financial:* sales, revenue, profitability, margins, share price, and market cap.
2. The second set is *customer metrics:* customer acquisition, customer satisfaction, customer retention, and growth of existing accounts.
3. The third is productivity *metrics:* Quality metrics, safety/incident numbers, rework, on-time shipments, new product introductions, and online departures for an airline.
4. Finally, executives spend some time on *human capital metrics:* leadership competency, employee engagement, and turnover/retention. In many organizations, the fourth item will be the first to be thrown overboard when times get tough.

You may recognize these four different sets of business metrics from our conversation on culture in Chapter 6. If your organization has adopted the Balanced Scorecard methodology, then this structure will also look familiar. With the Balanced Scorecard, executive teams develop the discipline of running the business on more than just financial metrics alone. They measure progress against a number of variables, tracked to a set goal. For each item, there is a direct

- Objective
- Target

- Measure
- Initiative(s) to help reach the target

In the Balanced Scorecard method, the four areas of focus are typically called Customer, Financial, Process, and Learning & Growth. All of the metrics are interrelated. Some interrelations are more obvious than others and easier to measure, but to recall Einstein's quote, there are many hard-to-measure relationships still having a strong organizational impact.

Consider these four data sets. How much consideration does each of these get in your organization?

We would argue that these four sets of metrics form a critical dashboard for a balanced perspective in any contemporary enterprise and that an inability to focus and manage all four will result in lower levels of performance.

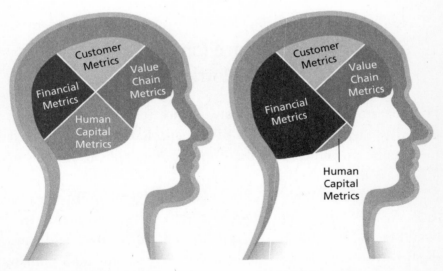

Does an executive's brain in your enterprise represent a balanced view?

Or is the focus primarily on the financials?

Yet the leadership team of any given organization tends to have a bias for one set of metrics over the other. This is sometimes due to the nature of their business (i.e., customer focus in retail, operational in airlines) or the point in the company's life cycle (i.e., rapid start-up growth versus going out of business profitably).

The amount of mindshare each one of these is granted is a reflection of—and an impact on—the company culture. Senior managers very quickly learn which of the four will get them the most recognition when positively affected, and consequently the metrics being tracked will drive behavior.

In many enterprises, the *people* set of metrics is delegated to the HR team and barely makes the scorecard or executive dashboard of metrics that matter.

One of first steps in committing to an engagement initiative (or securing executive buy-in) is to make room for human capital metrics on your routine monitoring process.

The Importance (and Lack) of HR Metrics

HR departments, problematically, do not tend to be as metrics driven as, say, finance, sales, or IT. Where they do collect data, it tends to be a patchwork of disconnected and duplicitous pools of information.

HR leaders always talk about getting a voice in the organization's decision-making process. A first step in achieving this would be to hire business analysts in their department and have them to run correlative studies between the company's human metrics—and the business performance by division, site, or geography.

Experian

This was the experience at Experian, the data management firm whose core business is monitoring, tracking, and protecting credit scores and other consumer information.

It was the comparison and correlation analysis of engagement scores, financial results, and NPS that allowed Experian's technically minded executives to realize the importance of engagement. There is now a growing appreciation that engagement is a major contributor to a purposeful culture and to delivering financial results.

Experian did not conduct an ROI study; instead it introduced engagement numbers from its survey into each department's key metrics, allowing the company to demonstrate a correlation between high-performing departments and high engagement. This correlation was enough for even the most cynical leaders at Experian to buy into to the process.

Nomura

Nomura, the Japanese financial services giant, manages its entire HR function based on core metrics.

To help build the process, Nomura recruited a business analyst from McKinsey & Company to develop an HR dashboard. Today, the organization reports to the board on some 20 key performance indicators that are meticulously tracked and reported.

"You have to somehow demonstrate the value added in hard numbers," says Awedhesh Krishna, the global head of HR for Nomura. "Otherwise, why would the CEO and CFO buy into any HR initiatives? Many HRDs will go straight to the money saved on recruiting as a result of reduced turnover, but there are many other compelling metrics you can track."

"Every profession has a language," says Krishna. "And often it is a very technical language. This is true in banking, finance, and engineering. HR has to learn the language [of these other functions] and the required numeracy in order to communicate and sell its own value. HR often fails because of this shortfall on communication."

Quantitative, Qualitative, and Mixed Measurement

There are many aspects of the human side of an enterprise (such as culture) that are difficult to measure objectively or directly. Unlike money in the bank or number of units produced, you are dealing with perceptions, emotions, behaviors, and feelings. Such intangible items do not lend themselves to straightforward quantification. Nor is there a regulatory obligation to track these numbers.

While many consulting firms will claim to provide highly reliable and validated instruments for measuring employee engagement (or satisfaction or culture), in reality these approaches only provide a snapshot in time and are riddled with problems of definition, implementation, and interpretation.

At the same time, an organization can produce a lot of useless data as part of its routine reporting. We mentioned that HR can be lacking in useful metrics. This is true. Yet HR functions can generate large volumes of *incidental* data (metrics that just happen to be measurable and are already available) such as average age and tenure of employees, percent of employees with advanced degrees, days of training, sick time/PTO (personal time off), number of hours at work (a surprising metric, given how people work from home early in the day and at night), and diversity ratios.

It's easy to hang your hat on this information just because it exists and is easily available, but in truth it has little value in an engagement effort. This six, quadrant analysis is how leaders should organize the data that they compile:

	Less useful in correlating engagement to your business outcomes	**More useful in correlating engagement to your business outcomes**
Readily available	Don't let this distract you or drive your thinking. Keep it as peripheral at best.	Add to your score card.
Not currently reported but can be generated with some additional effort	Don't invest effort in generating reports off this.	Consider investing the effort, but prioritize carefully.
Not practically measurable	Ignore.	Include only as soft data and collect anecdotally

A Mixed Approach

To get a complete picture of the impact that employee engagement has on performance, it is best to use a multifaceted approach in which quantitative data from several sources (financial, operational, customer metrics) is complemented with qualitative information. This will include one-on-one interviews, small focus group sessions, and rolled-up qualitative feedback from managers using simple online journaling-type platforms. The increasing use of internal social media platforms or strategic rewards programs can also add a particular richness to the picture.

Three Measurement Points

Your metrics dashboard will rely on measuring progress at three stages:

1. Measuring business metrics—build out the four dimensions (financial, customer, productivity, and human capital)
2. Measuring engagement levels or, in the absence of a formal engagement survey, tracking other metrics you can use as a proxy to gauge employee satisfaction and contribution
3. Measuring engagement drivers and the activities undertaken to affect the drivers

The specific metrics that you choose should depend on your business strategy (pick metrics that are at the heart of your operation), the initiatives you have underway (measure those activities closely), and your analysis of available metrics from the preceding six-quadrant analysis.

Engagement Drivers	Engagement Levels	Business Metrics
(Survey data on engagement drivers or measures of activities undertaken to increase engagement)	*(Engagement levels determined by a survey or other metrics that may reflect engagement levels)*	*(Metrics you use to manage your business)*
Survey scores for items that are leading indicators	**Survey scores that are lagging indicators (e.g., engagement levels)**	**Financial and productivity metrics: Revenue and profit per employee**
Or alternative metrics like:	*Or alternative metrics like:*	Employee turnover
Use of career initiatives (career days, career conversations, portal deployment)	Applicants per external job posting referred by employees	Customer satisfaction/service/retention
		Number of accidents reported

Engagement Drivers	Engagement Levels	Business Metrics
Internal communication campaign metrics	Applicants per internal job posting	Absenteeism, sick days
Number of individual (one-on-one) engagement conversations completed	Best places to work participation	Quality measures
	Attendance (attendance tracking, cars in car park, computer log data)	*Other metrics may be department specific:*
Number of purposeful job rotations and promotions		Number of orders processed in customer service
Number of team engagement conversations completed and senior leader feedback received	Leadership assessment scores	Number of help desk issues satisfactorily closed in IT
	Employee participation rates (social media, staff events, community service)	Number of project milestones or NPI steps completed in R&D
Tracking of initiatives based on last round of engagement survey	Innovation process: the number of suggestions per month	
	Time spent in meetings	
Training of workforce on roles and responsibilities for engagement	Number of formal employee complaints	
	Training sign-ups	

By establishing such a dashboard and tracking progress over time, you will have a set of metrics upon which you can gauge progress. While this may not be a strict ROI analysis, it is sufficient in our experience to credibly measure your progress given the complex factors at play in any sizable organization. Your goal is to be able to say, "We are doing these things to impact employee engagement, we have seen evidence of increased engagement, and these business measures have improved as a result."

Takeaways

- Demonstrating a cause-and-effect relationship between increases in engagement and bottom-line business results is difficult, expensive, and probably useless.

- It is important that you have agreed on the purpose of creating a more engaged workforce—what immediate (and measurable) business metrics are you chasing? They are ones that are trackable and should be expected to trend with increases in engagement.

- You can include specific metrics in your Balanced Scorecard or business dashboard and ensure your engagement efforts are on track by using carefully selected variables as indicators of business performance.

11

The Good, the Bad, and the Ugly of Engagement Surveys

Surveys: A Love/Hate Affair

We have touched on the topic of surveys repeatedly throughout this book, and by now you might be under the impression that surveys are a waste of time. They are not. They have become the starting point for many companies who want to address the issue of employee engagement. Through the years we have seen many organizations chase survey scores and lose sight of why they are surveying in the first place. Increased short and long-term productivity is the prize—not the survey scores—and increased productivity can be achieved without a survey. There are many other alternatives for organizations that want to start to address engagement without spending money on surveys.

Before jumping in with a survey, you should also consider: Are you really prepared for the feedback you are going to get? Are you committed to act upon that feedback?

Twenty-four percent of employees are engaged at North American companies where the employees report that surveys were conducted but no visible follow-up occurred. *This is three percentage points lower than engagement levels at companies that did nothing at all, suggesting that surveying without follow-up can actually damage engagement levels.* If your organization is unable or unwilling to act on the insights gleaned from a survey, don't do the survey at all. You may lose credibility with your employees.

Although surveying without follow-up can backfire, there is another approach guaranteed to lower your employees' engagement levels: pay lip service to engagement. In our study, fewer than 2 in 10 (19 percent) employees who reported seeing "a lot of talk, but no action" are fully engaged. Nearly 1 in 3 of those individuals (32 percent) is actually disengaged. Managers who wax lyrical about the importance of engaged employees or promise to act on engagement issues can severely damage their team's contribution and satisfaction if they fail to walk the talk.

Best practice is a 12-month cycle (with meaningful activities in between) that should tie to a company's scorecard metrics. It can take three full cycles (measure/share results/take meaningful action) to get to a stage where the organization is hitting its stride and has a meaningful internal baseline to compare against. That's a three-year commitment to get the process right.

If you don't have the appetite for three organization-wide survey cycles, consider alternative ways of gathering insights on engagement in your organization:

- Smaller pulse surveys
- One-on-one meetings or team-based conversations with upward aggregation of themes/suggestions
- Intranet-based chat boards or social media
- Small team meetings/luncheons with semi-structured conversation
- Exit interviews

If you are going to go the survey route (or if you are considering revisiting your current survey process), here are some best practices and pitfalls to avoid.

A Pinch of Salt. . .

Given the complexities of mapping the entire organization, collecting responses, and reporting, it is possible you will experience some noise in the system. Large organizations are in a state of permanent flux. Between the survey going out and the data getting reported, some managers will have changed roles; some departments may have merged.

One problem that this moving target presents: it makes it easy for managers to be dismissive of the data because they believe it is not statistically valid. We have heard many times, "This survey was conducted before we restructured. Things are different now."

Another reason for being conservative: engagement surveys are subject to bias. It is challenging to account for all factors that may introduce bias into the data, even with the most validated instrument. A survey will never give you data that is exact, up to the moment, and unbiased. It should be seen as directional. The data may be lagging slightly compared to where your department is today. But if you examine its high-level trends, themes, and perspectives, the information can still be extremely useful and informative.

Getting It Right the First Time

Many organizations engage in their first survey with great enthusiasm and high expectations, only to fall flat on their faces. Running large surveys across the entire enterprise is logistically complex and fraught with potential pitfalls.

Yet very few executives or core teams, tasked with the surveys, consider starting small and working their way up. They typically insist on eating the whole enchilada in one sitting.

Consider Celebrity Cruises, a subsidiary of Royal Caribbean Cruises Ltd. (RCCL). Jay Rombach, the company's associate vice president, Human Resources, describes the challenges of learning how best to survey its specific employee populations.

As a service organization, RCCL understands the importance of employee engagement. The company was eager to develop an effective survey process but faced a few challenges. Ninety-five percent of Celebrity's employees are on the open seas, and cruise lines are 24/7 operations. Another major issue was that for many of Celebrity's employees, English is a second language.

"Before 2006, Celebrity ran a traditional satisfaction survey with 70 items," Rombach says. "The timing was not great, but we have only a few opportunities to get people to respond. We ended up doing it before people left on vacation and many didn't understand some of the questions."

Eventually Celebrity adopted a shorter survey and focused on engagement. They changed survey formats, survey questions, and survey processes, opting for monthly measurement shipboard. It took several months and survey cycles to fine-tune a process that worked for them.

Today that persistence is paying off. "Engagement now has the attention of our CEO and board of directors," says Barbara Kallay, vice president, Human Resources Business Support for RCCL. "Our CEO, Richard Fain, gets it. He has now requested that we include engagement as a key productivity metric, which we measure across our entire organization."

Characteristics of a Good Survey

Whether you design your survey in-house or use a third party solution, you want to ensure your survey is straightforward and practical. Here are some of the key characteristics to look for:

- Keep the survey short and resist the temptation to use the survey as a way to collect a lot of other data at the same time. As a rule of thumb, more than 35 items is too many.
- Your survey should be designed for the long term, permitting longitudinal studies over multiple survey cycles.
- The survey needs to answer in practical terms:
  - Who's engaged?
  - Who's not?
  - Why?
- The survey should help identify who is most at risk and what can be done to help them (e.g., what's driving/preventing satisfaction and what's driving/preventing contribution?).
- Use mobile technology: in this working environment of BYOD (bring your own device), you have the opportunity to give employees direct access to the survey via their smartphone, tablet, or home computer. With appropriate security,

most employees prefer doing this as a way to provide feed-back. It is also a great channel for encouraging spur of the moment feedback, to collect opinion on the ground—outside of the survey process.

- The final report must be clear and actionable! If the final report is more cross-tabs than conclusions and recommendations, it will be hard to take action.

Actionable Items

An obvious (yet one of the biggest) mistake we see when working with clients who have a previously established employee engagement survey, is that they are not using actionable survey items.

If you're going to survey, make sure that each item has a direct action that can be taken as a result of the data you collect. If you have not experienced the entire survey cycle, it can be difficult to truly grasp what items can be useful and which will be "interesting but useless."

Imagine: you distribute summary reports to a dozen managers after you have completed your survey analysis. After going over the reports each of these managers realizes that about half of the data (although insightful) isn't actionable. The items may be scientifically proven to correlate with engagement—but they are difficult to influence. Gallup's "Best Friend at Work" question is often criticized on this basis. It is statistically validated, but likely not something a manager can take action on.

If you're going to ask managers to hold action planning sessions with their direct reports, you need to provide them with data that they can act on and that fits within their span of control.

If You're Focusing on the External Benchmark, You're Measuring for the Wrong Reasons

We understand the desire for organizations to benchmark externally. We also understand that most organizations want to benchmark against other organizations that operate in the same industry. Indeed, we see many organizations take the very same approach to budgeting: if the industry norm is 6.5 percent of revenue dedicated to marketing, an organization questions why 7.1 percent is being spent. Employee engagement (like marketing) is not about keeping up with the Joneses. You need to determine a level of activity and a budget that is in line with your strategy.

But every organization in the world (regardless of industry) has its own unique culture and values, which shapes the organization's needs. Two similar companies in the same industry can operate very differently, making an external benchmark less valuable than establishing a internal baseline.

Do a Few Things Superbly

A good strategy involves selecting a few things to do very well, not trying to make changes using all of the levers at once. Blindly copying the practices of competitors is lazy and likely to fail as a competitive strategy. A good strategy also seeks competitive advantage by doing a few things superbly that competitors are not doing or are not doing well.

—*Dr. Gerry Ledford*

We will always recommend downplaying the external benchmark and instead focus on establishing an internal baseline for your organization. An external benchmark may be important in the early rounds of measurement to give your leadership team a sense of relative performance. But internal benchmarking is more useful when sharing the results with the organization.

Focusing on internal benchmarks instead of industry comparisons communicates to your entire team that your people are more important than what is going on inside other organizations, and that you won't settle for the industry norm. You've lost sight of what really matters if you're continuously comparing your organization to others.

Your own people's opinions are more important than any other organization's perspectives. They're telling you what they need to drive their engagement while you're focusing on what's driving other people's engagement in other organizations. See the disconnect?

As organizations become more sophisticated in their engagement strategy, they increasingly disregard external benchmarking in favor of internal longitudinal tracking.

Survey Best Practices Summary

- If you are not prepared to openly share the results and have a candid conversation around your survey data—warts and all—do not even bother with a survey. Choose other data-collection approaches.

- *Plan the entire survey cycle carefully before you initiate.* Do not have a core team run the project on a cross-that-bridge-when-we-get-to-it basis.

- *Share survey results quickly.* Even in a global multinational organization, you need to target six weeks from closing the survey to sharing results. You need to turn results around quickly and remove any barriers or delays such as manager communication or pushback from leaders who get bad scores.

- *Don't overanalyze.* A survey is just a snapshot in time—it will tell you the current state of play and key themes. Don't indulge in nitpicking or discussing the meaningful difference in sigma values.

- *Time the survey carefully.* Timing of the survey is also a strategic decision. Launching during or after a reorganization or right after bonuses are handed out may influence your data either positively or negatively.

- *Identify strategic job families.* Once the survey is sent, it will be too late to identify specific subgroups, so think carefully about what specific populations you want to study. They may not be identifiable by hierarchical structure alone. One company preloads performance ratings so that the engagement of high performers can be studied. Job families, strategic roles, or employees who joined via specific programs are all good candidates.

- Ensure that you have *senior leadership commitment to share the results* no matter what before the survey initiates. Don't accept a "let's look at the results, then we can decide" response. Set firm dates and solid commitments on when, how, and by whom the data will be shared."

- *Ensure that senior leadership and line managers take ownership of survey results.* This should not be seen as an undertaking owned (and acted on) by HR—they are simply the facilitators/administrators for the survey. As K. Ramkumar, executive director, ICICI Bank Limited, describes it, "In our communication we make it clear that this is not an HR process or the company's data—the data belongs to the employees. And so it is shared in complete candor and openness."

- Consider your overall budget for engagement activities and *right-size your survey*. At maximum you should spend one-third of the budget on data-gathering activities. Two-thirds should be dedicated to activities that improve the results and are sustainable (not just before or just after the survey takes place).

- *Plan logistics carefully*. Even small snags in data mapping or collection can throw off entire surveys. Ranbaxy Laboratories ran into such a snag when coding of paper responses got mixed up. "One division of 2,000 people ended up with 4,000 responses. From that point on, the data integrity was question-marked. We looked at the 15 drivers that Hewitt defined for us, but honestly at the time there was little action that would impact the scores, the actions were disjointed. The results were never cascaded," says Dr. Rakshita Sharma, director, global OD at Ranbaxy, who has since rectified Ranbaxy's survey process.

- Whether you select 6-, 12-, 18-, or 24-month intervals, plan the survey cycle at a tempo that *allows for effective action*.

- *Consider surveying contractors/consultants as well*, not just full-time employees. This may require a separate survey, but these people also contribute to your success.

- *If you are going through a period of rapid change and need quicker cycles, use pulse surveys*. When the CEO of HSBC bank needed to keep his finger on the pulse of the company during times of rapid change, the bank adopted a cycle of one global survey every two years and pulse surveys going out to one in four employees every quarter. The new cycle means that HSBC can track quarterly progress without imposing a major reporting burden on the organization. One pleasant surprise: while the biannual survey had a participation rate of 72 percent, the pulse surveys saw response rates of about 80 percent.

- *Communicate the objectives, timelines, what employees can expect, and what's in it for them before you start the survey*: show the math. Give people an opportunity to raise questions or concerns.

- *Equip the core team.* While your core team may be eager, they may need support and input from external experts especially if this is their first pass at the entire process. Too often core team members are there to represent their function/department but slow the process down because they don't invest the time to stay up to speed. Make sure core team members will prioritize this effort.

- *Equip managers.* Do not drop reports in managers' laps with no context or help on how to interpret the results. This is a critical step in ensuring buy-in and commitment to taking action.

- *Make sure the final report is easily understandable and includes conclusions and recommendations.* The goal is to drive committed action.

- *Ensure managers don't perceive their scores as a punishment*—even if their scores are painful to read. It's an opportunity to put things out in the open, and if positioned properly, managers will be grateful for the insights and the support. If positioned badly, it will be a temptation to game the system on the next go-round.

- *Plan some immediate high-visibility activities* in response to the survey, but *invest most of the time and effort into sustained activities over time.* Avoid creating to-do lists that managers need to complete once and then check the box (this is how the vast majority of post-survey action plans are viewed by managers).

- *Use the post-survey communication activities as another opportunity to clarify the key themes that emerged.* For example, flexible work conditions may come out as a key theme inhibiting engagement, but the meaning is open to interpretation. Does it mean that people want the ability to work remotely, the option of working in teams, more flextime, or simply to deviate a little from the fixed 8:30 to 5:30 schedule?

Roll Out the Results on Schedule

Communication from the top down is critical in an engagement initiative, helping to establish authenticity and build trust in senior leaders. Start from the very top and work the results down through the levels of leadership and management. The most senior leaders in an organization should be privy to the results of an engagement survey before everyone else. Conduct a summary presentation with senior leaders and then provide them with their respective data. Allow them an opportunity to read through and digest their data before providing lower level leaders and managers with their survey results. This controls for any sort of hurt feelings and minimizes the risk of rumor mills starting. But do not build in any approval or release points. Your communication schedule should be short, sharp, and planned ahead of getting the results. Leaders should receive their data, get the chance to reflect, and get support in interpreting the results. They should not be given the opportunity to halt the process while they decide whether or not to share the results. Think of this as the results of an election: everybody is entitled to see the final tally. Build in just enough time for leaders and managers to understand the feedback before moving to the next level.

Less Less and More More

We covered a long list of things to consider in preparing your engagement survey. The four biggest items are:

1. Less items (okay, *fewer* items)—keep the survey short.
2. Less benchmarking—focus on items specific to your organization, and keep external benchmarking in perspective.
3. More frequent: implement fewer enterprise-wide surveys—and more monthly or quarterly surveys that sample part of the employee population.
4. More strategic: as you refine your approach, focus on actionable items that are in line with your business strategy.

Do or Don't Tie Compensation to Survey Results?

We have seen many organizations tie compensation of senior leaders to the outcomes of the employee engagement or climate survey. At face value, the rationale is sound and supports the idea of creating a balanced leadership approach by putting emphasis on human rather than financial variables. Another good argument is that engagement scores are leading indicators of organizational health, whereas financial results are actually backward looking: a reflection of performance over the last quarter or the last year.

But this approach is an "advanced maneuver" that we only recommend to companies that are a few years into their engagement efforts and that have an established and reliable measurement process. In the same way that pure financial tracking of an executive's performance is sometimes known to drive unwanted behavior, tying compensation to engagement scores sometimes prompts leaders to game the system.

RCCL, however, has successfully linked a common engagement score to bonus compensation for some senior leaders.
According to Kallay, "This decision clearly demonstrates that
our senior leaders understand the linkage between engagement,
discretionary effort, and productivity." Rombach discusses how
it works:

> In the past there was no direct correlation between rewards
> for managers and performance. We've changed that to make
> a fairer promotion and compensation policy. We now have a
> real focus on getting alignment around variable compensa-
> tion based on core company performance metrics.
>
> Our bonus program is quarterly, to reflect real time data
> and outcomes. Employee engagement scores are collected
> every month, with a rolling sample of the workforce. Every
> month there is a report based on about 1,000 responses.
>
> The monthly report contains a series of graphs that
> include the overall engagement score for the month, year-
> to-date score, a breakdown of scores by ship and department.
> These reports go to each ship's steering committee (top five
> to six executives). The KPI is the overall engagement score.
> There is a healthy competition about these across the fleet.
> HR sends out emails listing the "highest score across the
> fleet." The data is very "real time." And the data gets used.
> Leaders know what their goals are with respect to employee
> engagement, financial performance, and guest satisfaction.
> It's not just about bonuses. Seeing engagement scores every
> month allows them to investigate drops in scores and make
> changes as appropriate. Leaders talk with their staff about
> engagement: "Where are the scores? What do we need to do
> to improve?"

RCCL has achieved the mindshare and sense of real-time
feedback it needs to improve performance, but not every company gets this right. If you decide to tie compensation or bonuses

to engagement scores, we recommend you first consider the following:

- Ensure your measurement process is established and reliable.
- Ensure that managers and senior managers understand how engagement is measured and what your organization's objectives are with regards to engagement.
- Ensure managers are clear on what aspects of engagement the bonus is being tied to.
- Only build in a bonus element for senior leaders who are in a position to influence the overall culture. If building in a bonus component for front-line managers, tie the bonus to the department or division's overall scores and not to that manager's immediate team scores.

What You Can Learn from Response Rates

Response rates can vary widely between companies, and can vary from one survey to the next but here are some broad parameters:

If you have a response rate below 70 percent, then you are looking at two scenarios:

1. Your employees are telling you something: they don't trust the process or the guarantee of anonymity, or they aren't taking it seriously. Never assume that low response rates indicate that people are satisfied and don't have a need to provide feedback. We have never seen this happen. (But we have heard executives speculate on this!)

2. Your survey process is broken and people are not getting the message, managers are dismissing the effort, or maybe the data

collection process is too complicated or cumbersome. The more questions you include and the longer it takes to complete, the more people are likely to abandon it mid-session.

If you experience low response rates, you need to do some digging. Assign someone to call individual managers and contributors. Check to see if they got the survey, if people were completing it, and if they had any questions.

If you have response rates between 70 and 85 percent, you are in the norm and you will have reliable results.

If you have response rates above 85 percent, you are in excellent shape.

If you have response rates in excess of 100 percent, your survey process is broken.

What to Expect on Subsequent Surveys

The response rates of subsequent surveys are a real acid test. In organizations where the process was diligently followed and where follow-up action was visible and sustained, we invariably see an uptick in the participation rate. Another factor here is that your core team running the survey will get slicker and smarter. Communication will improve, timelines will tighten, and managers will be open to encouraging their teams to respond.

If you did not follow up visibly on the first survey, you can expect participation rates to drop. We have seen drops from the mid-70s to the mid-50s in firms where no follow up took place.

Survey Pitfalls to Consider

- Gaming the system: depending on how the survey was positioned, managers may tell their teams to answer with a certain bias (and not always a positive one).

- Ignoring cultural bias: for example, there is a wide range among Europeans as to which ratings they use, and employees in some Asian countries are reluctant to provide negative feedback about superiors.

- Tying engagement scores to compensation before the survey process is well established (at least three cycles).

- Reading too much into the participation rate on the first two surveys: you should expect some mistrust on the first pass. The participation on the second round will increase if you do a strong follow-up after the first survey.

- Employees may use the survey to vent. It's part of the process, and venting always has a root cause.

Focus on Actions as a Result of the Survey, Not on the Survey Results Themselves

If your organization is full of highly analytical, data-driven technical professionals, it's likely that these individuals will want to see every possible cross-tabulation of your data set. They may even ask for individual reports of every manager underneath them on the organizational chart. It's good to have the desire to understand the data, but it can be detrimental to get stuck in the weeds. Understanding the corollary nature of the data may be useful in certain instances, but what's more efficient is to understand the data at a high level and then to take action as quickly as possible. Spending too much time analyzing creates a noticeable gap between the time the survey closed and the beginning of action planning. You have communicated a timeline to your organization, and it's important that leaders and managers stick to it. Deviating from the established roll-out plan may undermine your efforts to increase engagement throughout your organization.

Good Follow-Up Actions versus Bad Follow-Up Actions

Following a survey, you will generate a long list of actions on how to respond to the feedback. Remember, the survey is just one diagnostic tool in a larger process. The tail should not wag the dog. You should have a broader business strategy, a related OD strategy (that includes engagement), and you can use the survey to tell you if you're on track.

Plan some effective communication around the results and some visible activities to gain credibility that leadership is acting on the data. Don't pick transactional crowd pleasers as your visible actions. The items on alignment (assuming your survey included them) make for good starting points.

Then focus on the real meat of the effort: sustained activities that provide course correction and influence the culture. They need to address the core satisfaction and contribution drivers and should (if all goes well) look less like a knee-jerk reaction to bad survey scores—and more like rational organizational improvement initiatives.

These are initiatives that you probably would have undertaken in any case, but now you have the data to prove that these will have the most impact.

You need to stay focused. You are not going to be able to address each and every item that comes out of the survey, so pick a small handful. Choose three to five key items that you want to address—and build your plan around these. You won't be successful if you try to address the entire range of issues all at once. Pick the items that are the strongest drivers of satisfaction *and* contribution—these will have the highest likelihood of continued support. Then assign these purposefully to those managers that you need to have leading the effort. Resist the temptation of handing the assignments to the least busy team or the HR department.

Now you can explain to people why a process or business practice is changing—it is in response to employee feedback in the survey! You also have an opportunity to connect other organizational initiatives to the survey results, even if the activity was initiated independently from the engagement study.

For example, you may happen to be upgrading your internal job posting (IJP) process and the issue of career came up as an area of concern. Here is an opportunity to highlight the value of the IJP intranet. Highlight current and recent initiatives to demonstrate that the survey results have been understood.

Naturally, the actions you choose will be determined by the survey results. We have provided some examples of good and bad follow-up that we hope will illustrate the characteristics that you are looking for.

Good Follow-Up Actions

Activity	Why it worked well
Executive road show to share the results, but also to start to address some of the concerns and improvement suggestions. For example, employees may communicate that they do not quite get the new strategy, so the senior leadership double down on communication efforts.	The action was rapid after the survey. Employees felt that the survey actually prompted the senior leadership into action. Builds trust in the survey process. Plus having everybody get the strategy is really important!
In response to employees feeling they do not know what the other departments are doing, hold cross functional discovery days when each department hosts a booth in the cafeteria and showcases their current projects/key focus.	Was felt more as an employee-led initiative rather than a top-down assignment; in fact, senior leadership made a point of attending the internal trade show but kept a low profile. Became an annual event that was looked forward to by the entire staff.

Bad Follow-Up Actions (well intentioned, but misguided)

Activity	Why it backfired
Sharing survey results quickly with all staff without first briefing the managers.	Employees had lots of questions on next steps and interpretation of the data. Managers felt undermined and in turn dismissed the survey as unscientific.
Asking managers to pick one item from the feedback and take visible and rapid steps to show that the organization was committed to action.	What most employees experienced was a rash of uncoordinated activities at the team level with no consistency or coordination. Some manager-initiated activities ran counter to the activities of other groups.
Managers tasked with coming together in peer-discussion groups to share their findings and discuss department-level observations and trends.	The conversations did not generate additional actionable insights but took time to organize, delaying the process by several weeks. As a result, a lot of momentum was lost.

How to Increase Engagement without the Use of an Engagement Survey.

It seems to be a common misconception that an organization should run an employee engagement survey to kick off an engagement initiative. This is simply untrue. Yes, a survey helps you establish a baseline, but there are other metrics that you can use to analyze the level of engagement in your organization (e.g., customer satisfaction, turnover, labor complaints, employee accident reports, etc.; we discuss these in Chapter 10).

More important than establishing a baseline is taking action when you know that action needs to be taken. It doesn't take a survey for you to know that certain groups in your organization are either fully engaged or fully disengaged. Rather than spending time, money, and resources on a survey, it's often more efficient to put into place a structured engagement training regimen. If you plan on taking this approach, it is advisable to note where certain metrics are at pre- and post-training, so that you can analyze the trends in your data.

We recommend the following topics for individuals, managers, and executives, as explored in Chapters 4 and 8:

Individuals

1. How to take control of your own engagement
2. Personal values clarification that shapes satisfaction at work
3. Skills and development needs clarification to perform your best work
4. Career development
5. Alignment of individual interests with organizational goals

Managers

1. Fundamentals of employee engagement
2. How to hold one-on-one and team meetings to discuss drivers of contribution and satisfaction
3. How to coach teams and individuals to higher levels of employee engagement

4. How to create individualized engagement partnerships
5. How to apply engagement essentials in daily leadership

Executives

1. How to influence employees to care enough about their own engagement to take ownership of their engagement
2. Situational sensing and emotional intelligence
3. Inspirational storytelling—get the numbers down off the charts and into story form as to why it matters to you personally

Takeaways

- Surveys are an important tool in employee engagement initiatives, but too often end up driving activity rather than monitoring progress.
- If you do decide to survey, plan out the entire process carefully before you initiate.
- Avoid the many pitfalls of surveys.
- Consider alternatives, especially if your resources for taking action are limited.

12

Final Considerations

We have explored many facets of creating a more engaged workforce. Now let's summarize some of the most important recommendations, decisions, options, and pitfalls to consider. Engagement initiatives are complex, with a lot of moving parts. The best approach for you will depend on a host of factors, including where your organization is currently on its engagement journey. Therefore, we have grouped this chapter's content in three broad (and occasionally overlapping) categories:

- Where to start if your organization *does not* have an engagement initiative in place
- How to build on or fix *existing* engagement initiatives
- Important reminders that cut across timing and situations

We also hope this summary helps you as a reference when you return to this book looking for specific content in light of your current progress and area of focus.

If You Are Starting Out

If your organization has never tackled engagement, you have the opportunity to lay the foundation for an effective engagement strategy right from the start. (If you are already in the thick of engagement activities, read this section and ask yourself if your current approach is the best to achieve your goals.)

Guiding Principles

Here are some basic rules of the road to set you up for success:

- Make engagement about business results from day one. Not connecting a more engaged workforce to business outcomes is practically a guarantee that your efforts will be short-lived.
- Maintain a bias for action. It is easy to get caught up in the analysis and debate, but it is dialogue and action that move the needle.
- Start with (and reinforce) a common definition of engagement that focuses on both the needs of the individual and the needs of the organization.
- Remember that engagement is a personalized equation, which needs to be addressed at the individual employee level.
- You will be well on your way once engagement has become a daily priority and a shared responsibility of individuals, managers, and senior executives—and when organizational roadblocks have been removed.

Start with Purpose

With your company's business strategy in hand, start by analyzing your core business metrics. Ask yourself: Is the way our industry approaches employee engagement optimal? How should our approach differ?

Draw up an Engagement Vision Statement that captures your purpose and includes the following elements.

- A common definition and model of employee engagement that works for your organization
- Explanation of why employee engagement is important in your organization (e.g., productivity, customer satisfaction, increased sales)
- The philosophy that engagement is an individual equation and needs to be addressed at the individual (I) level (see Chapter 1)
- Roles and responsibilities for executives, managers, and individual contributors (see the IME/O model in Chapter 4)
- A vivid picture of what would be different in your organization if engagement levels were higher.

This final point helps your workforce visualize success, so invest the time (and involve others) in creating compelling, detail-rich examples for specific functions. Push the description beyond vague statements such as "Stores with higher engagement will see higher sales per square foot." Instead, aim for specifics such as "Stores with higher engagement will see a proportional increase in visits per month by existing customers, especially in departments with high customer interaction such as the deli counter and the pharmacy. When customers visit they will feel how different and welcoming our stores are. Every day on our

Facebook page we'll read about the exceptional experiences that customers have with our staff."

Secure Senior Leader Buy-In

Socialize your vision statement and the importance of engagement with senior leadership and gauge the response. You might think it is a great idea—but do your peers agree with you?

We describe best practice in gaining senior team commitment in Chapter 6. Here is a simple checklist to evaluate whether or not you have secured it.

Senior Leadership Commitment Checklist

- *Senior leaders in your organization are committed to being the torchbearers of employee engagement.* They are eager to present at town hall meetings, participate in organization-wide action plans, include key engagement metrics on internal dashboards, and weave engagement into every communication. They keep the topic of engagement on their personal agendas instead of delegating to a second-in-command.

- *Senior leaders communicate candidly regarding engagement data and in a timely manner.* A good acid test for senior leader commitment: If their scores are not favorable, how do they react? Do they brush them under the table? We have seen some organizations include employee engagement scores in their annual CSR or annual shareholder reports when progress looks positive, only to omit them when they turn the other way.

- *Senior leaders provide resources beyond the cost of the diagnostic to drive engagement.* When times get hard, the investment in regular measurement, training, and support is sustained.

- *Senior leaders take control of their own engagement and model behaviors with their immediate teams.* Remember that disengagement in the C-suite is likely to derail efforts. The senior team must demonstrate high levels of engagement.

- *Senior leader compensation is linked to engagement activities and scores.* As mentioned in Chapter 11, this can be effective but needs to be approached carefully (as in the RCCL example) because it can lead to unwanted behaviors.

Commitment of Other Interested Parties   To be successful, who else do you need on your side? Take a quick assessment of your organization's readiness to tackle engagement. Are there other key stakeholders or interested parties whose commitment is required to make your initiative work? How will you get them involved?

Examples could include

- Board members
- Volunteers
- Union representatives
- Adjunct networks
- Critical suppliers or subcontractors

Consider Running a Pilot

You don't need to tackle your entire enterprise at once. Consider starting engagement efforts in one plant, one country office, or one division. Even organizations that approach engagement across the board rapidly realize that some departments make progress faster than the others—typically thanks to some evangelists on that team who keep engagement firmly on the agenda and prove its value in building the business.

If you do run a pilot, you need enough data to make your proof of principle credible and learn lessons you can apply for a larger implementation. You may not have the organization-wide survey data you would like, but there are many other measurement approaches you can take (see Chapter 10 and tips later in this chapter). Be sure to pick a metric that will carry weight—this may be a sales metric if your company has a sales culture, a customer support metric that is readily available, or any metric close to the company's strategy (such as more rapid turn-around of software releases or progress to key milestones in pharmaceutical research).

And make sure you pick a metric that you can monitor over time and that will not be discredited easily. Collect data on your core metric(s) before and after your engagement efforts.

If the pilot does not give you the results you were expecting, interview the staff and learn from the effort. If the employees didn't benefit from the initiative, find out why. If they did benefit, ask why you didn't see the results you wanted. Were the managers focusing only on satisfaction at the expense of contribution?

Assemble a Core Team

Your initiative will need senior team support and a wide network of champions to help guide and sustain your efforts. You will also need a core team that represents the key stakeholders of engagement and can invest time in creating and managing the overall initiative. Think of your core team as the nerve center for engagement operations, and the individuals who will keep senior leaders and the rest of the organization up to speed on the initiative.

Select team members based on the engagement champion criteria we presented in Chapter 6. They need expertise, dedicated time, credibility, influencing skills, senior leader support and access, and necessary resources. Team members should also have strong project management capabilities, partnering skills for communicating day-to-day with any external providers, and a solid understanding and passion for employee engagement.

Be aware of individuals who may join simply to gain representation on the project but who are not necessarily committed to its success. While you may need to accommodate certain stakeholders, make sure each member of the core team will commit sufficient time to the effort and will not slow down the process with the specific agenda of his or her department or division.

The head of the core team is typically the head of the champion network. This is not compulsory, but frequently the logical set-up since the required characteristics are the same.

Improving Existing Engagement Initiatives

If your organization has been running engagement surveys, this section contains ideas for ratcheting up your efforts. If you are starting out, the ideas and actions in this section are valuable, too. We have grouped them together here because they represent activities that many organizations have not tried.

Equip People

As described in Chapters 4 and 6, individuals, managers, and executives need to understand what engagement is (and why it is important), be clear on their accountabilities, and be willing and able to take on the roles the organization needs them to play in creating a culture of engagement.

Companies often budget large amounts for the annual survey but little to nothing for equipping people to pursue engagement every day. If you are serious about moving away from a disappointing cycle of survey administration, communications, and action planning, then you need to budget two to three times the cost of your survey on training and tools for your workforce.

A Note about Onboarding and Career Transitions As new employees come on board or as employees move into new roles, educate them on their accountabilities with respect to engagement. Individuals need to understand from day one that they own their engagement equation. New managers should hear the expectation that they must CARE about engagement (as explained in Chapter 4) and have the chance to develop the appropriate coaching skills if they are transitioning from individual contributor roles. Executives, too, need to explore how to create an environment that fuels engagement.

Too often the responsibility falls to human resources alone, but successful onboarding and career development programs have input from every level of the organization's thought leaders.

Align Practices

What practices currently run counter to your engagement effort? Interview or survey managers in various departments to find out. You can enroll the support of your Six Sigma team if you use that methodology. Changing organizational practices is often hard work. Pick your battles and secure some high-impact, high-visibility wins early on.

Make sure from the offset that you have some credible metric to show that the practice change delivered results. Even oblique measurements of the impact will do: one top airline in Asia Pacific uses the number of customer complaints sent to the CEO as a key metric. The airline determined that most complaints were about service interactions, and that engaged employees tended to have better interactions with customers. While not as quantitative as other forms of customer satisfaction or engagement studies, this metric reflects the number of people who were so frustrated that they took the time to look up the name and address of the CEO and write a letter or e-mail.

Develop Engagement Champions

The development of engagement champions (as described in Chapter 6) is something that needs to occur in parallel with other activities. This valuable network needs to be developed and fostered over time.

From a sequencing perspective, the only note here is that if you are investing in a large survey, you also need to invest time in identifying and training your champions before the next survey kicks off. Champions need to be in place to help drive participation. Then they should support the cascading communications of findings and train or support managers to take action.

Drive Action and Accountability with Frontline Team Meetings

Do not be fooled by the brevity of this little section. Frontline team meetings are one of the most value-added steps in any engagement initiative. *Whether you conduct a survey or not, run the frontline team meetings and process discussed in "Team Actions" in Chapter 6 (page 131).* These sessions are at the heart of the conversation that teams should be having around engagement because they focus day-to-day engagement strategies. They also set the context for one-on-one conversations that explore employees' individual engagement drivers and managers' coaching plans.

These meetings will provide you with the three elements of a team's agreements:

1. Actions the team commits to take
2. Actions the manager commits to
3. Insights and observations on factors that support or hinder engagement, which can be shared with senior leaders and human resources

If your managers record the meeting agreements online, you will be able to access reports that contain valuable insights and actionable items. A simple word cloud tool such as www .wordle.net can help you tease out themes and trends.

Revisit Your Measurement Strategy

The following is a brief synopsis of the decision points on measurement. Much more information is provided in Chapter 10.

What metrics are you going to put on your scorecard? You will need to plan your budget appropriately. Don't assume you need to jump in at the deep end with a full-on enterprise-wide survey. Your efforts can be far more targeted than this.

You may wisely decide that budget/commitment is not sufficient to both run a survey and invest time and money into initiatives that move the needle. Ask yourself which is most important: engagement scores (but no budget "to move the needle"), or money and resources you can use to improve engagement (but no data)?

The truth is, either of these could be your best bet in terms of gaining further commitment to take your initiative to the next level. It will depend on your company's culture and the style of the senior leadership team. But engagement surveys tend to be the approach of getting attention via bad news ("Employees don't trust us!"), whereas investing in making an improvement is a way of getting attention by demonstrating potential—typically a more positive approach.

Your Internal Dashboard   You have developed items that are reliably measurable and directly related to the company strategy. Now make sure these items are on the senior team's radar by including them in regular dashboard metrics or Balanced Scorecard items.

Beware short-lived business metrics. Too often people set off with good intentions, but the measuring and reporting activity itself slips and the numbers no longer get generated and reported. Even if no activity or progress has been made on the engagement initiative, develop the discipline of generating and reporting on the metrics. Keep the initiative on the agenda.

Survey Essentials   You probably already have a lot of quantitative and qualitative data: most 360-degree leadership assessments will give some measurement of attributes that tie to engagement such as trustworthiness and inspiration; exit interviews of departing employees; what people say during town hall meetings; customer feedback; your own situational sensing when you walk around your headquarters building or travel to remote offices.

If you decide to go the full-on survey route, you need to do a lot of careful planning before setting anything in motion.

What follows is a typical 21-week timeline for a survey process. It is based on $T = 0$ being the day you open the survey. T indicates time in weeks, so your first step at $T-7$ means seven weeks ahead of the survey launching. Most organizations will find a 21-week schedule challenging, especially on their first survey. Your specific schedule will flex from this one based on the complexity of your organization—for example, administration of multiple languages or a large number of paper surveys may require more time.

Plan out your entire survey cycle *before you start*, including communication steps pre-, during-, and post-survey. Gain commitment to these steps before you know the results, do not allow executives to delay if the results give them pause, and do not expand the gap between data collection and results more than absolutely necessary.

T −7   Bring the core team together. Plan the survey, carefully map the organization structure to reflect your reporting requirements. Invest the time to plan your survey, but also the communications and commitment to follow up, no matter what the results.

T −5   Clarify executive roles and responsibilities, set dates for follow-up.

T −4   Identify and train engagement champions in their overall roles and responsibilities.

T −2   Communicate the plan and the purpose to the entire organization. Communicate specifically with managers to set expectations on their roles and follow-up.

T0–T4   Run the survey. Send reminders. Generate reports. Hold core team debriefing.

T5   Review results with the executive team. Confirm organizational action plans. Get executive commitment.

T6   Run sessions with engagement champions to review the data and discuss how best to share with the organization. (If champions are new, also train them in the role they need to play in training and supporting managers.) Let the organization know the results are compiled and share the plans for rolling out the results.

T6–T8   Prepare managers on the fundamentals of engagement and how to interpret reports. Provide each manager with his or her team findings. Senior leaders get their immediate team numbers and a separate report on their entire department/section.

T7–T10   Roll out the executive roadshow and conduct virtual town hall and site/division meetings (all communications to large teams) as appropriate.

T9–T11 Managers conduct team meetings to discuss findings and identify actions for increasing engagement levels of the team.

T10–T12 Managers conduct one-on-one engagement conversations to explore each team member's drivers of satisfaction and contribution as well as ideas for working together more effectively. Core team collects feedback from all levels of the workforce via interviews and online reporting tools (if appropriate).

T12 Follow up on organizational action plans to demonstrate accountability and momentum. Managers hold themselves and team accountable for local action items. Continue to check online reporting tool if available.

T13 Report back via core team on key metrics and qualitative feedback.

T14 Communication from top executive(s) and engagement champions highlighting progress, sharing compelling success stories, and reinforcing continued commitment.

Manager Preparedness for Handling Survey Findings Many managers feel like they are caught unawares when presented with survey results, especially in the first year (for them personally or for the enterprise as a whole). You can mitigate a manager's surprise through training and communication (we talk about this in Chapter 6 under "Step 3: Equip People").

You will know if managers are ready to receive, interpret, and act upon the results if

- Managers are trained and are confident to interpret their workgroup reports (using sample reports or actual data if timing allows).

- Managers feel prepared to hold team meetings to discuss findings and develop action plans at the workgroup level (using simple discussion guides and reporting format).

- Managers are equipped and committed to conducting one-on-one engagement conversations with team members to discuss their personal engagement equations.

Pulse Surveys   Pulse surveys can be an efficient way to monitor engagement levels and the success of your engagement efforts quarter-to-quarter. Many organizations are discovering the value of shorter pulse surveys, sampling either a subset (20 to 25 percent) or their entire employee population at a time.

For more details on pulse surveys, refer to "Step 5: Measure Progress" in Chapter 6.

Manager and Employee Focus Groups   First of all, if you are tempted to use focus groups to provide additional qualitative information to your quantitative data, give it careful consideration.

While focus groups seem like a reasonable approach, they are typically expensive (if using outside resources), do not generate candid information, are time-consuming, and generally don't provide the value or insights you are looking for. As a general course of action, we would not advise using focus groups. Still, companies do tend to utilize these either in the run-up to the survey to shape items or in the post-survey phase to validate and build on the findings in the survey data.

If you do decide that they have a role in *your* initiative, then be aware that there is no specific schedule or sequence for running focus groups for managers or employees.

There is one area where focus groups provide value: Having senior leaders run small group sessions on engagement during site visits or departmental reviews. With this approach you can keep the engagement dialogue going and reinforce the message that this is high on the corporate agenda.

Focus group sessions typically take 90 minutes and are conducted by two leaders (a facilitator and a note taker). Group composition can be determined by a number of factors—a good starting point is three to four cross-functional sessions (including new employees, tenured employees, and managers alike).

The Non-Survey Route for Data Gathering Here is a list of activities you can conduct to gain insights into engagement levels *and* take action to increase engagement—without conducting an employee survey.

1. Find alternative metrics and feedback collection method (manager survey, focus groups).
2. Socialize idea with managers. Be explicit on accountabilities.
3. Train managers on employee engagement fundamentals and conducting engagement conversations.
4. Have managers conduct group discussion similar to the survey debrief, but without survey data. (See "Team Actions" as detailed in Step 6 of Chapter 6 on page 131.)
5. Managers conduct one-on-one meetings with all direct reports.
6. Managers follow up with team to summarize the outcomes of all the conversations. Managers log and report action plan (via an online portal or other roll-up mechanism).
7. The core team reviews all feedback from all teams.
8. Results are shared by the senior leadership team, and visible actions are taken.

A Few More Cautions for Both New and Established Initiatives

Beware the Obvious Options

Core engagement teams often jump to some obvious fixes in response to their findings:

- Fix rewards and recognition
- Fix compensation
- Fix managers
- Fix the performance management system
- Fix career development tools and processes

None of the above fixes are quick. In fact, they can become black holes for the organization's resources. It is a common pitfall to jump on to initiatives like these, believing they (and they alone) can fix your engagement issues. They cannot, and often get shelved in the face of more pressing business priorities. Construct a careful engagement strategy and consider the multiple facets of the engagement equation. At the end of the day, the issue is addressed on the ground by equipping individuals, managers, and executives.

Avoid Analysis Paralysis

Too many organizations end up gathering and analyzing data, consulting with external experts, running focus groups, discussing engagement at employee events—but not actually doing anything to move the needle.

A core objective of your initiative should be to equip individuals, managers, and executives with the context, the model, and confidence to discuss and address engagement. All the other activities—from senior team commitment-building to surveying—are steps toward enabling that shared responsibility and daily priority.

Maintaining Momentum

You can't check off a box on your to-dos and conclude your engagement initiative is done. Instead, keep cultivating a culture of engagement with the following actions.

- Revisit your Engagement Vision: is it still aligned with your strategy?
- Is the senior team still on board, still aligned?
- Are managers maintaining their commitment to making engagement a daily priority?
- What success stories can you tease out and share?
- Is your core team operating all year round or simply coming together to administer the survey?

Appendix

Chapter 2: Great Days at Work

When we talk about engagement, it is easy to get caught up in dry data and terminology like *drivers, levels, benchmarks,* or *correlations.* But for you, as an active member of the workforce, employee engagement often plays out as *more great days at work.* Great days, as Chapter 2 explains, are wins for both you and your employer.

This quick activity will help you translate what *fully engaged* means to you. It will provide a visual that you can use to remind yourself of the work experiences that are most satisfying.

1. Think of a *specific* great day at work.
    - What were you doing?
    - Where were you?
    - With whom?
    - What did you accomplish?
    - How did you feel?
2. List five adjectives or phrases that describe that day. These descriptors provide insight into your values, preferred job conditions, and talents that you enjoy using on the job.

3. As you take control of your engagement, look for projects and roles that will provide opportunities to recreate the feelings of that great day.

4. If you have time, ask a colleague to complete the first two steps above and then compare notes. You may find that your great days look different, but there are common themes in the way you sum them up.

Chapter 5: How Engaged Are You?

Take your own engagement pulse regularly so you can ensure that you are prepared to lead your engagement initiative. To do so, think about the questions below. Then, based on your knowledge of the five levels of engagement we discuss in Chapter 2, mentally plot yourself on the model.

1. Consider your satisfaction:
   - How did you feel about coming to work today?
   - How well are your top values being satisfied by what you do?
   - Are you getting to do what you do best each day?
   - Does your work "work" for you?
2. Consider your contribution:
   - How clear are you on organizational priorities?
   - Are you focused on what matters most to the organization?
   - What stands in the way of maximum contribution?
   - Does your work "work" for your employer?
3. Identify where you are on the engagement model. (How does this compare to where you were last week?)

4. If you're not at the apex of full engagement, what can you do about it? Consider:

   • What do you have control over?

   • What can you start to do about this?

   • How can you change your own words and actions to become more engaged?

   • How can you change aspects of your job?

   • Whom can you enlist in positive change?

Chapter 5: Identifying Your Top Personal Values

Values are personal. But you don't leave them at home when you head for work. They travel with you, shaping your decisions, your actions as a leader, and your job satisfaction. Clarifying your personal values—what matters to you—helps you define success on and off the job. A firm values framework gives you a sharper sense of self-identity (you know who you are), greater self-assurance (you know where you stand), and clearer self-direction (you know what you want).

The process below will help you gain clarity on the things that you value. You'll need a piece of paper or computer to record and review your notes.

1. Take a few moments to think back through each decade of your life at work and outside of work. Start with your childhood! List a few of the most significant incidents in each decade. Any of the following examples could be considered *significant:*

   • Distinct markers of life—like the birth of a child or a promotion at work.

   • An event not particularly dramatic or significant by anyone else's standards, but the fact that you remembered it indicates its importance—for example, a particularly satisfying personal achievement.

   • Events in your life when you may have formed your own principle instead of merely subscribing to the rules, values, or beliefs of those around you (like your parents, peers, teachers, or managers). They may have involved stretching boundaries, challenging rules, disappointing someone's expectations, or acting on a belief to which you had only given lip service previously.

   • Incidents you did not initiate, but which left some profound or lasting impression on you.

2. Then consider the questions below. You need not write answers to each. Simply use them as triggers to recall notable events to add to your list.

   • What were your proudest moments?

   • When were you most frustrated, angry, defeated, or resentful?

   • When did you think a lot about a situation at work after hours and/or talk about it with friends or family?

- When were you most inspired?
- When were you most challenged?
- When were you most disappointed or confused?
- When did you feel most exhilarated, happy, or satisfied?
- When were you most filled with conviction or resolve?

3. Now, for each experience you listed,
   - Look for clues (obvious or subtle) about what was important to you in that incident. In hindsight, what value or view did you adopt or appreciate more fully as a result?
   - Record the value next to the experience. (Be sure to make the distinction between a lesson or reaction, and a value. For example, if the incident was: "A colleague with whom I'd worked hard on a project took credit for the success of the project," your reaction could have been, "I'll never trust him again." The value that was reinforced, however, may have been integrity, recognition, or collaboration.)

4. Review your notes (and your Great Day at Work notes if you completed the first activity in the Appendix). What is most striking to you? What themes do you see? Taking those themes into account, what are the five things that matter most to you? Those are your top values.

Chapter 5: Alignment with Your Values

Sometimes things feel out of whack. As you juggle responsibilities at work and home, it's easy to get swept up in activities, allowing external forces dictate your actions. It's up to you to make sure you're living your life in alignment with what's most important to you. When you do, you achieve greater satisfaction on and off the job.

Complete the following process for each of your top values.

1. On a scale of 1 to 10, with 1 being not at all and 10 being totally, rate how well this personal value is being satisfied.

2. Now consider the things at work and in your personal life that are contributing to satisfaction of this value *and* those things that are reducing satisfaction of this value.

3. Consider what you can start, stop, or continue doing to capitalize or build on the things that are satisfying this value.

4. Consider what you can start, stop, or continue doing to minimize or eliminate the things that reduce satisfaction of this value.

5. Take appropriate action.

Chapter 5: Do Your Current Job Conditions Support Your Best Work?

Jobs in themselves are neither satisfying nor dissatisfying. Two people in identical jobs can feel very differently about them because they have different values, interests, and talents. Ideally, your job should offer conditions under which you do your best work—and thrive. There may be some things that you will never be able to change. Other aspects of your job may represent low-hanging fruit that, if altered, can increase your satisfaction and contribution.

Periodically, take an objective look at what you like and don't like about your job. Decide what you'd like to change. Then take action. The following exercise will get you started.

1. Create a current job profile by selecting the appropriate option in each pair of statements to describe your current job.

	Highly describes ← → Highly describes	
1	Flexible work hours	Well-defined work hours
2	Attention to detail required	Big picture, conceptual focus required
3	High level of decision-making authority	Limited decision-making authority
4	Considerable contact with external customers	Little contact with external customers
5	Frequent communication with manager	Infrequent communication with manager
6	Work closely with others; teamwork and collaboration needed	Work mostly alone; independence needed
7	Low risk, low likelihood of failure	High risk, high challenge
8	Lots of travel, overnights	Little travel, rarely out of the local area
9	Frequent new assignments; quick turnarounds	Projects with long time frames
10	High visibility to senior management	Low visibility to senior management
11	High structure; goals and procedures established by others	Low structure; I establish my own goals and methods
12	Manage people; team leader	Does not manage people; independent contributor

2. Star (*) the job condition that most supports your satisfaction and contribution.

3. Circle the condition that most interferes with your satisfaction and contribution.

4. Consider:

   • What can you do tomorrow to maintain the condition you starred or change the condition you circled?

   • What do you need to maintain or change to create an environment in which you do your best work?

   • What do you want to maintain or change to ensure job satisfaction?

Chapter 6: Do Your Executives Create a Culture that Fuels Engagement?

Your success in creating a culture of engagement depends on your executives' commitment and abilities. This checklist can help you determine where to start in building the leadership capability you need.

Think about the majority of senior leaders in your organization and consider the extent to which you agree with each statement below . . .	Strongly Disagree				Strongly Agree
They are passionate about high performance and results.	1	2	3	4	5
They are passionate about high employee satisfaction.	1	2	3	4	5
They do what they say they will do.	1	2	3	4	5
They often talk about organizational values or guiding principles.	1	2	3	4	5
Their behaviors align with organizational values or guiding principles most of the time.	1	2	3	4	5
They communicate honestly.	1	2	3	4	5

Think about the majority of senior leaders in your organization and consider the extent to which you agree with each statement below . . .	Strongly Disagree				Strongly Agree
They communicate the organization's direction and priorities clearly.	1	2	3	4	5
Their communications are inspiring.	1	2	3	4	5
They talk about what employee engagement is—and why it is important.	1	2	3	4	5
They think about business results *and* employee engagement when they make decisions.	1	2	3	4	5
They speak to business results *and* employee engagement when they communicate decisions.	1	2	3	4	5
They let themselves be known on a personal level, beyond their title or role.	1	2	3	4	5
They link the work of the organization to a larger purpose.	1	2	3	4	5
They make sure employees know they are valued.	1	2	3	4	5
They celebrate significant individual and team accomplishments.	1	2	3	4	5

Scoring: Count the 4s and 5s above. Don't add them. Enter your total here.

*This profile contains 12 of the 25 items contained in BlessingWhite's standard Job Conditions Profile. Copying and distribution is prohibited without express written permission from BlessingWhite, Inc.

# of 4s and 5s	Grade
12 or more	**Don't relax.** Your leaders beat most of those we studied. But it takes a lot of work to sustain culture. Continue to hold them accountable. Support them.
7 to 11	**Look for trends.** Do your leaders struggle with similar leadership actions (e.g., communication)? What can you to do address these gaps? Whose support do you need?
6 or fewer	**Don't despair.** What department or business unit could lead the way? Where can you get traction to build on successes? Which leaders believe in engagement? Leverage them.

This profile contains 12 of the 25 items contained in BlessingWhite's standard Job Conditions Profile. Copying and distribution is prohibited without express written permission from BlessingWhite, Inc.

Chapter 7: Communication Tips

The following questions provide a useful springboard for preparing written communications or in-person opening comments for kicking off an engagement initiative. The headings or sequence are by no means the way "it ought to be done," just one way of organizing your thoughts to capture your workforce's hearts and minds.

Where Are We?

- What are the most important organizational goals right now?
- Why is the alignment of individual and organizational interests or engagement important to achieving those goals? (See Engagement Vision Statement content in Chapter 10.)
- What is our vision for the organization's future? How will this engagement effort help us achieve our long-term vision?
- What do we really mean by "engagement"?
- How does this engagement initiative align with other critical efforts?
- Why do I believe this engagement initiative will be valuable, from a business standpoint, for *each employee*? (Refer to data/goals, stories of the impact engaged employees have on customers, etc.)

Why Am I Here (as a Leader)?

- Why do I believe this process will be valuable, from a personal standpoint?
- What have my own experiences been? (Share observations on your own work experiences and challenges, periods of

high/low engagement, personal stories about meaning at work, etc.)

- What are my own hopes and expectations for the workforce now?

What Am I Asking of All of You?

What do I need each of you to do? For example:

- Put aside cynicism?
- Really participate?
- Be thoughtful?
- Be candid?
- Talk to your manager?
- Talk to your team?
- Continue to take accountability for your professional success?
- Continue to partner with your manager?
- Think of this focus on engagement as a win-win for your managers and you, so that you end up on same page regarding your success, their success, and the organization's success?

Ten Actions for Becoming a Coach

The following is taken from BlessingWhite's research report "The Coaching Conundrum" (available online at http://www.blessing white.com/research). It summarizes the best practices for managers who seek to build greater engagement through coaching.

■ ■ ■

When we asked survey respondents to think of their best coach—and then think of the one coaching action by that manager which they most valued, two responses stood out: "stretched me beyond what I thought I could do" (20 percent) and "asked questions to help me think through and solve work challenges on my own" (18 percent).

This is good news for the 30 percent of managers who said their biggest challenge was "not having all the answers." It turns out that most employees do not want advice or a set solution.

Will your team members remember you as a best coach? Here are 10 tips for becoming a manager for whom coaching is a way of life.

1. *Be clear on your goals and your role.* Get clarification now if you do not know how your team's priorities fit into the organization's larger goals. And pay attention to what coaching is not, listed later.

2. *Hire coach-able, stretch-able employees.* Successful coaching is a partnership. Explore coach-ability in selection interviews, finding out from candidates past experiences with coaching. Where did it have the most impact? When and why did it not work out previously? You may also want to include questions that uncover how candidates feel about challenging situations and learning new skills.

3. *Get to know each team member.* Every employee comes to work with unique values, aspirations, experiences, and talents. Andrew Coven, director of engineering at Adobe Systems, emphasized the need to tailor coaching approaches based on what you know: "I treat everyone differently. I want to capitalize on people's strengths. Coaching also has to have a relevant context. It is very specific to the work that

employees are doing. One size does not fit all when it comes to coaching."

4. *Coach the individual, not the demographic.* This is a slight variation on the preceding comment. Generational data is useful for understanding the different lenses through which the workforce sees life and work. But when it comes down to coaching, an employee's values and goals are influenced by more than their age; coaching relationships are built on one-on-one pairings, not aggregate trends.

5. *Tell team members what you expect of them.* Thriving coaching partnerships require joint accountability. Employees need to ask for help, listen to feedback, provide candid upward feedback, and follow up on agreements.

6. *Coach for increased engagement.* You can—and should—keep both satisfaction and contribution in mind as you coach your team members (the proverbial win-win solution). Angie Brayshaw, worldwide employee engagement director in London for American Express Technologies Group, explained that her firm, which had a strong focus on performance coaching, has tried to focus more on engagement to sustain their success: "It is not just enough to coach for performance against the company's goals. We want our managers to coach around career goals and be more in tune with the personal aspirations and interests of individuals."

7. *Ask more questions.* The more questions you ask, the less likely you will fall into micromanaging or irrelevant advice. Questions help you provide a sounding board for employee ideas. They can also provide the stretch that employees want from coaches. Questions can unlock potential, as Maria Del Busto, global chief human

resources officer for Royal Caribbean Cruises Ltd., suggests: "We're all creatures of habit. Asking questions is a great way to help people identify and work on areas that are holding them back—often things that they're not even aware of."

8. *Delegate effectively.* Paul Konstantos, national work cover manager at integrated facilities management organization, Sodexo Australia, made this point: "In recent months I have made a concerted effort to focus on delegating tasks to allow time dedicated to coaching. The benefits are not only realized in bottom-line results and an improved culture. I help individuals achieve personal growth." Another reason to delegate: it sets clear expectations and goals. It is a lot more motivating to help employees learn how best to reach an agreed-to destination, rather than having to clarify what you wanted in the first place.

9. *Ask for feedback.* Do your coaching actions help or annoy your team members? You cannot use performance as your only metric. It is possible that your efforts are damaging employee morale. Tom Pucciarello, program management authority at BAE Systems, described such a situation: "In talking to one manager and direct report, I learned that the manager thought he was doing a great job coaching—adding a lot of value. Unfortunately, the direct report felt it was a waste of time and that the manager was only interested in giving advice."

10. *Don't take that coach hat off.* Whether you think of this as looking for coaching moments or employing a coaching leadership style, the message from successful leaders is to coach continuously. If you have established individualized, trusting partnerships, coaching conversations become easy.

Coaching Is Not...

- *An event.* Coaching is an effective way for managers to lead and communicate with their direct reports. Managers interact with their employees on a regular basis; it just takes a little effort, thought, and practice, to turn these routine interactions (in person or on the phone) into coaching moments.

- *A discrete tactic for performance problems only.* Coaching is a way to groom high performers for new opportunities, create succession planning, get work done most productively, and keep people excited about their work and the organization. When coaching is happening in every interaction, e-mail, and meeting, managers can have significant impact on their team's employee engagement and the organization's success.

- *A one-size-fits-all approach.* For coaching to have a positive impact, managers must flex their coaching style to respond to the unique needs and talents of each team member. The best coaches develop a systematic approach that clarifies and responds to the unique needs of each employee.

- *Advice.* Although managers may occasionally need to supply the right answer, more often than not, coaching involves helping team members think through situations and formulate their own solutions.

- *Something you do to employees.* Coaching requires joint accountability and a partnership. It is not a set of skills

(Continued)

for managers to apply or direct at their team members. Employees must be invited in as partners in the coaching process and be willing to receive and give feedback, share needs and interests, and request specific coaching as needed.

Interviews and Contributors

The authors would like to thank the many business leaders, academics, and consultants from around the world who contributed to this book. All contributed to broadening our thought leadership on this topic. The perspectives and insights of many of these individuals are quoted directly.

Karen Aaron, Technologist Specialist, Clinical Laboratories, Maimonides Medical Center and member of 1199 Union (Brooklyn, NY, US)

David Asplund, CEO, Lime Energy (Skokie, IL, US)

Michelle Auer, Senior HR Business Partner & Country Head of Human Resources, Zurich Financial Services (Sydney, Australia)

K.S. Bakshi, VP of Human Resources, IndiGo Airlines (Delhi, India)

N. Balachandar, Group Director of Human Resources, Café Coffee Day (Bangalore, India)

Louise Baxter, CEO, Starlight Foundation (Sydney, Australia)

Abhijit Bhaduri, Chief Learning Officer, Wipro (Bangalore, India)

Angie Brayshaw, Employee Engagement Director, American Express Technologies Group (London, UK)

Pam Brier, President and Chief Executive Officer, Maimonides Medical Center (Brooklyn, NY, US)

Phil Cameron, CEO, Innogence (Sydney, Australia)

Andrew Coven, Director of Engineering, Adobe Systems (San Jose, CA, US)

Paul C. Darley, President & CEO, W.S. Darley & Co. (Chicago, IL, US)

Judhajit Das, Chief of Human Resources, ICICI Prudential (Mumbai, India)

Maria Del Busto, Global Chief Human Resources Officer, Royal Caribbean Cruises Ltd. (Miami, FL, US)

Steve Dolan, Senior Director of Leadership, Organizational Effectiveness, Juniper Networks (Southbury, CT, US)

Dr. John Evans, CEO, Cultural Imprint, (Sydney, Australia)

Marshall B. Farrer, Managing Director, Australia/New Zealand, Brown Forman (Sydney, Australia)

Alexis Fink, Director of Talent Management Infrastructure, Microsoft Corporation (Seattle, WA, US)

Dee Fischer, Director of Organizational Development, Razorfish (Philadelphia, PA, US)

Matthew Froggatt, Chief Development Officer, TNS (London, UK)

Wissam Hachem, Head of Emiratisation & Corporate Development, Etihad Airways (Abu Dhabi, UAE)

Mark Hales, Director of Mission, St Vincents & Mater Health (Sydney, Australia)

Pat Hasbrook, Senior VP, Experian (Costa Mesa, CA, US)

Ann Huang, Senior HR Manager/Director, Red Star Macalline (Shanghai, China)

Derek Irvine, Vice President of Client Strategy and Consulting for Strategic Recognition, Globoforce (Dublin, Ireland)

Lorraine Jacomelli, Learning and Development Advisor for Global Marketing and Supply, GlaxoSmithKline (Slough, UK)

K S Jamestin, Director Human Resources, ONGC (New Delhi, India)

Barbara Kallay, Vice President, HR Business Support, Royal Caribbean Cruises Ltd. (Miami, US)

Paul Konstantos, National Work Cover Manager, Sodexo Australia (Melbourne, Australia)

Dr. Brenda Kowske, Senior Analyst, Bersin & Associates (Minneapolis, MN, US)

Awdhesh Krishna, Managing Director and Global Head of HR, Nomura Bank (Powai-Mumbai, India)

Mardi LePage, CEO, URSA Clemenger (Sydney, Australia)

Tony Ling, VP of Human Resources, Dianping.com (Shanghai, China)

Adil Malia, Group President Human Resources, Essar (Mumbai, India)

Rodney Miller, former dean, corporate university for FPL Group (West Palm Beach, FL, US)

Steve Miranda, Managing Director, Center for Advanced Human Resources Studies (CAHRS) at Cornell University (New York, NY, US)

Paul Mitchell, Executive Coach and CEO of The Human Enterprise (Sydney, Australia)

Alain Moffroid, Vice President of Customer Development, Unilever (Sydney, Australia)

David Norton, former Company Group Chairman, Johnson & Johnson (Princeton, NJ, US)

Terry Pearce, author and executive coach, founder and President of Leadership Communication (San Francisco, CA, US)

Tom Pucciarello, Program Management Authority, BAE Systems (Boston, MA, US)

K. Ramkumar, Executive Director, ICICI Bank Limited (Mumbai, India)

Andrew Reeves, CEO, George Weston Foods (Sydney, Australia)

J. Thomas Richardson, Senior Vice President and Infrastructure Strategy/Architecture Executive, Bank of America (Denver, CO, US)

Keith Rodwell, Group Executive, BOQ Finance (Sydney, Australia)

Jay Rombach, Associate Vice President, HR, Celebrity Cruises (Miami, FL, US)

Tony Sablo, Senior Vice President, Human Resources, The National Geographic Society (Washington, DC, US)

Sandra Sadowski, Director of Spa and Fitness, The Ritz-Carlton New York, Central Park (New York, NY, US)

Daniel Sarkadi, Sales Director, General-Providencia (Hungary)

Dr. Rakshita Sharma, Director, Global OD, Ranbaxy Laboratories (Delhi, India)

Daryl Sisson, Head of Direct Asia, Thomson Reuters (Sydney, Australia)

Dr. Riana Smith, Vice President Performance, Learning & Development, Etihad Airways (Abu Dhabi, UAE)

Dr. David Spicer, Senior Lecturer in Organizational Change and Head of Human Resources Management Group, Bradford University School of Management (Bradford, UK)

Michael Stilp, CEO, Equigroup (Sydney, Australia)

Shellene Tan, GMHR, Equigroup (Sydney, Australia)

Vikram Tandon, Head of Human Resources, HSBC Bank (Mumbai, India)

Johnny Taylor, CEO, Thurgood Marshall College Fund (Washington, DC, US)

Pam Tracy, Organizational Development Consultant, DST Systems (Kansas City, Mo, US)

B. Venkataramana, India Senior Vice President and Chief People Officer, Landmark Group (Bangalore, India)

Endnotes

The content of this book was assembled based on years of ongoing research and insights gathered from working with companies around the world. During this period, BlessingWhite published a number of research reports that informed our perspective and helped evolve our thinking. These reports, several of which are referenced here, can be downloaded from http://www.blessingwhite.com/research.

Preface

1. Despite Experian's initial "leap of faith," they continue to refine their approach and monitor the relationship between engagement and business metrics, as detailed on page 223.
2. The unbroken world record for spinning multiple plates, verified as a Guinness World Record, is held by David Spathaky, assisted by Debbie Woolley, who spun 108 plates simultaneously in Bangkok, Thailand, on television in 1996. He had previously held and broken his own record four times since 1986.
3. Bersin & Associates, "Employee Engagement: A Changing Marketplace," 2012.

Chapter 1 What Is Engagement Anyway?

1. Frederick Herzberg's *Harvard Business Review* article "One More Time: How Do You Motivate Employees?" first published in 1968, presents his motivation-hygiene theory of job attitudes and job enrichment. Hygiene factors are clearly associated with the "What have you done for me lately?" syndrome.

2. Herzberg, in his discussion of motivation, described motivation factors of achievement, recognition, the work itself, responsibility, promotion, and growth. These factors remain important to employee engagement today.

3. BlessingWhite's "Employee Engagement Report 2011" provides more detail on the links between engagement levels and intent to stay.

4. Brenda Kowske, "A Snapshot of the Employee Engagement Industry," Bersin & Associates, March 30, 2012. www.bersin.com/blog/post/A-Snapshot-of-the-Employee-Engagement-Industry.aspx

5. BlessingWhite's "Employee Engagement Report 2011" revealed that career development and training was a top engagement driver of employees in nearly every region worldwide, across generations, functions, and levels of engagement.

6. The 2011 BlessingWhite report also indicated that less engaged employees desire greater clarity on organizational priorities, while more engaged employees selected more resources as the factor that could most increase their contribution.

7. BlessingWhite's "Leading Technical Professionals Report" identified six needs that expert employees exhibit with more frequency and intensity than nontechnical employees. Needs in addition to keeping current include autonomy, achievement, professional identification, participation in mission and goals, and collegial support and sharing.

Chapter 2 The Five Levels of Engagement

1. BlessingWhite's global 2011 study revealed that 52 percent of employees could be categorized as neither fully engaged nor fully disengaged. In some regions of the world or particular functions, it was as high as 60 percent. A 2011 Gallup Daily tracking survey calculated that 71 percent of American employees fell in that zone.

2. BlessingWhite, "Employee Engagement Report 2011."

3. BlessingWhite, "Employee Engagement Report 2011."

Chapter 3   Global Insights and Macro Trends

1. In June 2011, Mr. Asplund took the role of executive chairman of the board. See www.lime-energy.com/about/leadership/david-asplund.

2. Gartner, Inc., "Gartner Says Worldwide BPO Growth Continues Despite Mixed Fortunes in Developed Countries," August 22, 2011, http://www.gartner.com/it/page.jsp?id=1772115.

3. Eileen Appelbaum, Annette Bernhardt, and Richard J. Murnane, eds., *Low-Wage America: How Employers Are Reshaping Opportunity in the Workplace* (New York: Russell Sage Foundation, 2003).

4. Mac McClelland, "A Day in the Life of a Warehouse Wage Slave," *Week*, May 18, 2012, http://theweek.com/article/index/228096/a-day-in-the-life-of-a-warehouse-wage-slave.

5. See Phillip Dampier, "PBS Documentary: Subcontracting Cell Tower Work Has a Human Toll," Stop the Cap! May 24, 2012, http://stopthecap.com/2012/05/24/pbs-documentary-subcontracting-cell-tower-work-has-a-human-toll/.

6. Silke Januszewski Forbes and Mara Lederman, "The Role of Regional Airlines in the U.S. Airline Industry." http://weber.ucsd.edu/~sjanusze/www/book_chapter_oct06.pdf

7. "Flying Cheap," *Frontline* documentary written, produced and directed by Rick Young, www.pbs.org/wgbh/pages/frontline/flyingcheap/

8. Pew Research Center, "Millennials: A Portrait of Generation Next," February 2010, http://pewsocialtrends.org/files/2010/10/millennials-confident-connected-open-to-change.pdf.

9. Brenda Kowske, "Just the Facts about Millennials (And How Organizations Are Supporting Them)," Bersin & Associates, November 17, 2011, www.bersin.com/Practice/Detail.aspx?id=15013.

10. Pew Research Center, "Millennials."

11. Pew Research Center, "Millennials."

12. BlessingWhite, "BlessingWhite Employee Engagement Report 2011," www.blessingwhite.com/research.

13. Bureau of Labor Statistics, "Employee Tenure Summary," September 14, 2010, www.bls.gov/news.release/tenure.nr0.htm.

14. Transparent Consulting, "Transparent Consulting Employee Engagement Index," www.transparent-consulting.com/engagement-index/.

15. Bill Taylor, "Why Zappos Pays New Employees to Quit—and You Should Too," *HBR Blog Network*, May 19, 2008, http://blogs.hbr.org/taylor/2008/05/why_zappos_pays_new_employees.html.

16. Saurabh Sinha, "Kingfisher Airlines Market Share Lowest in Country," *Times of India*, April 18, 2012, http://timesofindia.indiatimes.com/business/india-business/Kingfisher-Airliness-market-share-lowest-in-country/articleshow/12709142.cms.

17. Interglobe Technologies, "Awards & Recognitions," 2011, www.igt.in/aboutus/IGT-awards.html.

18. The blue paper, "China's Educational Development Report 2009," released by the Social Sciences Academic Press at the Chinese Academy of Social Sciences, a major government think tank (www.cssn.cn/), says women who have received higher education suffer less gender discrimination at work.

19. U.S. Bureau of Labor Statistics (BLS).

20. Gallup Business Journal. (http://gmj.gallup.com/content/122849/employee-engagement-labor-relations.aspx)

21. Jessica Tyler, "Employee Engagement and Labor Relations,", *Gallup Business Journal*, http://businessjournal.gallup.com/content/122849/employee-engagement-labor-relations.aspx.

22. Ian Griggs, "Death of the Working Men's Club, *Independent*, August 10, 2008, www.independent.co.uk/news/uk/this-britain/death-of-the-working-mens-club-889632.html

Chapter 4   Shared Accountability and Daily Priority

1. For the hoax story, see Lawrence Tabak, "If Your Goal Is Success, Don't Consult These Gurus," *Fast Company*, December 31, 1996, www.fastcompany.com/magazine/06/cdu.html. For the Harvard connection, see Sid Savara, "Writing Down Your Goals—The Harvard Written Goal Study. Fact or Fiction?" http://sidsavara.com/personal-productivity/fact-or-fiction-the-truth-about-the-harvard-written-goal-study.

2. Barry Z. Posner and Warren Schmidt, "Values Congruence and Differences between the Interplay of Personal and Organizational Values Systems," *Journal of Business Ethics* 12 (1993): 172.

3. James M. Kouzes and Barry Z. Posner, *Leadership Challenge*, 3rd ed. (San Francisco: Jossey-Bass, 2002), 51.

4. BlessingWhite, "Employee Engagement Report 2011."

5. BlessingWhite, "The Coaching Conundrum 2009."

6. The core principles of CASE were first introduced by Rob Goffee and Gareth Jones in their book *Why Should Anyone Be Led by You?* Goffee

and Jones' thought leadership has informed much of BlessingWhite's work with senior leaders.

7. Goffee and Jones, *Why Should Anyone Be Led by You?* (Cambridge: Harvard Business School Press, 2006), 195.

8. Terry Pearce, *Leading Out Loud: Inspiring Change through Authentic Communication* (San Francisco: Jossey-Bass, 2003).

Chapter 5   A Dead Battery Can't Jump-Start Another

1. According to BlessingWhite's research, 52 percent of vice presidents or above worldwide are engaged compared to 24 percent of individual contributors and 30 percent of managers. There are variations by region in the size of the difference between executive engagement and the workforce at large, but the pattern is clear: engagement levels are higher at the top of organizations.

2. Evan Williams's Twitter blog, October 4, 2010, http://blog.twitter.com/2010/10/newtwitterceo.html.

Chapter 6   Culture

1. William H. Mobley, Lena Wang, and Kate Fang, "Organizational Culture: Measuring and Developing It in Your Organization," *Link*, Summer 2005, www.ceibs.edu/link/latest/images/20050701/1394.pdf.

2. Adapted from Christopher Rice, "Driving Long-Term Engagement through a High-Performance Culture," in *Building High-Performance People and Organizations*, ed. Martha I. Finney (Westport, CT: Praeger Perspectives, 2007).

3. More than 100 HR professionals were polled by BlessingWhite at a 2012 TriState SHRM conference.

4. Theory X represents a negative view of human nature that assumes individuals generally dislike work, are irresponsible, and require close supervision to do their jobs. eNotes, "Theory X and Theory Y," www.enotes.com/theory-x-theory-y-reference/theory-x-theory-y.

5. Pearce, *Leading Out Loud*.

6. Kenneth W. Freeman, "To Create Long-Term Shareholder Value, Start with Employees," *HBR Blog Network*, http://blogs.hbr.org/cs/2011/10/to_create_long-term_shareholde.html.

Chapter 7   Seems Kind of Obvious: Align Your Employees!

1. The feedback and discussion planning process of *Managing Personal Growth (MPG)* is designed to uncover disconnects in how managers and employees perceive work priorities. The 1 in 3 estimate is based on nearly 40 years of program facilitator observations, client data, and hundreds of thousands of program participants.

2. Goffee and Jones elaborate on communication vehicles in *Why Should Anyone Be Led by You?*

3. Pearce, *Leading Out Loud*.

4. For more on organizational values clarification check out Rice's "Driving Long-Term Engagement through a High-Performance Culture" (www .blessingwhite.com/content/articles/DrivingLongTermEngagement ThroughaHighPerformanceCulture08.pdf) and David S. Pottruck and Terry Pearce's book *Clicks and Mortar: Passion-Driven Growth in an Internet-Driven World* (San Francisco: Jossey-Bass, 2000).

Chapter 8   Dialogue and Empowerment Trump Action Planning

1. BlessingWhite, "Employee Engagement Report 2011."

2. The Thurgood Marshall College Fund (TMCF) is named for the U.S. Supreme Court's first African American justice. It was established in 1987 and supports nearly 300,000 students in the United States.

3. BlessingWhite, "Employee Engagement Report 2011." This correlation with engagement level is stronger than an effective working relationship like "I work well with my manager." In the study, the item about working relationship correlated with engagement levels but not as strongly as "I know my manager well as a person."

4. Goffee and Jones, "Know and Show Yourself—Enough" in *Why Should Anyone Be Led by You?*, page 29.

5. BlessingWhite's "The State of the Career 2007" report revealed that the majority of employees want interesting or meaningful work and work-life balance more than they want a promotion.

6. Kim Lamoureux, "Strategic Onboarding: Transforming New Hires into Dedicated Employees," *Bersin & Associates Research Bulletin* 3, no. 1 (January 4, 2008).

7. Michael Watkins, *The First 90 Days* (Cambridge, MA: Harvard Business School Press, 2003).

Chapter 9 Career Development

1. BlessingWhite, "Employee Engagement Report 2011."
2. BlessingWhite, "The State of the Career 2007" www.blessingwhite.com/research.
3. BlessingWhite's "State of the Career" research indicated only 45 percent of employees know what they want their next job to be.
4. James O'Toole and Edward E. Lawler III, *The New American Workplace* (New York: Palgrave Macmillan, 2006), page 219.
5. Report released by the Partnership for Public Service in 2012 (a non-profit organization that studies U.S. federal workplace issues) entitled "Mission-Driven Mobility."
6. BlessingWhite, "The State of the Career 2007."
7. BlessingWhite, "Leading Technical Professionals Report," 2006.

Chapter 10 Measuring ROI

1. Adapted from Robert S. Kaplan and David P. Norton, *The Balanced Scorecard: Measures that Drive Performance* (Harvard Business Press, 1996).

Chapter 11 The Good, the Bad, and the Ugly of Engagement Surveys

1. BlessingWhite, "Employee Engagement Report 2011." Also summarized in the article "The Good, the Bad and the Ugly of Employee Engagement Surveys," BlessingWhite eNews Article, October2010 http://www.blessingwhite.com/enews.

Index